108 PLACES YOU MUST VISIT IN SEATTLE

From Hidden Gems to Iconic Landmarks, Discover the Incredible Emerald City!

JACK ELSON

ISBN: 978-1-962496-04-9

For questions, please reach out to Support@OakHarborPress.com

**Please consider leaving a review!
Just visit: OakHarborPress.com/Reviews**

Copyright 2023. Oak Harbor Press. All Rights Reserved.

No part of this book may be reproduced or transmitted in any form or by any means, electronic or mechanical, including photocopying, recording, or by any other form without written permission from the publisher.

FREE BONUS

GET OUR NEXT BOOK FOR FREE!
Scan or go to:
OakHarborPress.com/Free

TABLE OF CONTENTS

How to Use This Book 1
Seattle's History 3
    Food and Culture 4
Bars & Nightclubs 5
    Unicorn 6
    Rhein Haus Seattle 7
    Q Nightclub 8
    Cha Cha Lounge 9
    Deep Dive 10
    The Crocodile 11
    The Hideout 12
    mbar 13
    The Botanicale 14
Parks 15
    The Seattle Center 16
    T-Mobile Park 17
    Lumen Field 18
    Gas Works Park 19
    Kerry Park 20
    Warren G. Magnuson Park 21
    Green Lake Park 22
    Olympic Sculpture Park 23
    Discovery Park 24
    The Klondike Gold Rush National Historic Park 25
Museums & Galleries 27
    Chihuly Garden and Glass 28

    The Museum of Flight 29
    The Museum of History & Industry (MOHAI) 30
    Seattle Art Museum 31
    Seattle Aquarium 32
    Museum of Pop Culture 33
    National Nordic Museum.. 34
    Pacific Science Center 35
    Seattle Children's Museum 36
    Seattle Asian Art Museum 37
    Seattle Pinball Museum 38
    Burke Museum of Natural History and Culture 39
    Wing Luke Museum 40
    Henry Art Gallery 41
Famous Buildings & Structures 43
    Space Needle 44
    The Spheres... 45
    Fremont Troll 46
    The Seattle Great Wheel.. 47
    Suzzallo and Allen Libraries 48
    Sky View Observatory at Columbia Center............................ 49
    Pike Place Market 50
    The First Starbucks 51
    King Street Station 52
    The Fremont Rocket 53
    The Gum Wall 54
    Seattle Center Monorail 55
    Seattle Public Library, Central Library 56

- Districts ... 57
  - Pioneer Square ... 58
  - Capitol Hill ... 59
  - South Lake Union ... 60
  - Queen Anne ... 61
  - Chinatown-International District ... 62
  - Ballard ... 63
  - Belltown ... 64
- Beaches ... 65
  - Alki Beach ... 66
  - Mount Baker Beach ... 67
  - Madison Park Beach ... 68
  - Seward Park ... 69
  - Matthews Beach Park ... 70
  - Golden Gardens Park ... 71
- Festivals & Annual Events ... 73
  - Bumbershoot Festival ... 74
  - Seafair Festival ... 75
  - Folklife Festival ... 76
  - Día de Muertos Festival Seattle ... 77
  - Emerald City Comic Con ... 78
  - Lunar New Year Fair ... 79
  - The Seattle International Film Festival ... 80
  - Seattle Latin Dance Festival ... 81
  - The Seattle Improv Festival ... 82
  - Indigenous People Festival ... 83
  - Festival Sundiata Black Arts Fest ... 84

- Seattle Queer Film Festival 85
- Northwest Flower & Garden Show 86
- Children's Film Festival 87
- The Seattle International Auto Show 88

Zoos & Animals 89
- Washington State Ferries 90
- Woodland Park Zoo 91
- Debbie Dolittle's Animal Encounters 92

Theaters 93
- Seattle Opera 94
- Seattle Rep 95
- Seattle Children's Theatre 96
- The Seattle Public Theater 97
- Seattle Symphony 98

Other Fun Attractions 99
- Bruce Lee and Brandon Lee Grave Sites 100
- Jimi Hendrix Grave 101
- GameWorks Seattle 102
- Haunted History Ghost Tours of Seattle 103
- Burke-Gilman Trail 104
- Ballard Locks Fish Ladder 105
- The Seattle Waterfront 106
- Seattle Chocolate 107
- Bill Speidel's Underground Tour 108
- The Seattle Japanese Garden 109
- The University of Washington Campus 110
- Seattle Shakespeare Company 111

Seattle Wine Tours 112
Pacific Northwest Ballet 113
Seattle Whale Watching Tours 114
Seattle Free Walking Tours 115
The Center for Wooden Boats 116
Hot Tub Boats 117
Moss Bay 118
Proper Planning 119

How to Use This Book

Welcome to your very own adventure guide to exploring the many wonders of the city of Seattle. Not only does this book offer the most wonderful places to visit and sights to see in the vibrant city, but it provides GPS coordinates for Google Maps to make exploring that much easier.

Adventure Guide

Sorted by region, this guide offers over 100 amazing wonders found in Seattle for you to see and explore. They can be visited in any order and this book will help you keep track of where you've been and where to look forward to going next. Each section describes the area or place, what to look for, the physical address, and what you may need to bring along.

GPS Coordinates

As you can imagine, not all of the locations in this book have a physical address. Fortunately, some of our listed wonders are either located within a National Park or Reserve, or near another landmark. For those that are not associated with a specific location, it is easiest to map it using GPS coordinates.

Luckily, Google has a system of codes that converts the coordinates into pin-drop locations that Google Maps can interpret and navigate.

Each adventure in this guide includes GPS coordinates along with a physical address whenever it is available.

It is important that you are prepared for poor cell signals. It is recommended that you route your location and ensure that the directions are accessible offline. Depending on your device and the distance of some locations, you may need to travel with a backup battery source.

Seattle's History

Before the arrival of pioneer settlers in 1851, Seattle was the home of the Coast Salish peoples, most notably the Suquamish and Duwamish tribes. This area was their homeland for thousands of years, and they developed an extensive network of trade there. These tribes still live in the Seattle area today.

When white settlers arrived in the area, their first settlement was named New York-Alki. Shortly after this townsite was developed, the settlers moved across Elliot Bay to what is known as the historic Pioneer Square district today. It was in this area that they found a protected deep-water harbor. This new settlement was named Seattle in honor of Sealth, a Duwamish Native American leader.

The principal economic driver of the settlement was the lumber mill that Henry Yesler established in 1853. Much of the lumber produced went to San Francisco. Seattle attempted incorporation between 1865 and 1867, but the initial attempt was a failure. It was finally a success on December 2, 1869.

At the start of the 1870s, the Northern Pacific Railway Company extended the end of the line to Tacoma. Seattle followed by building a line to meet this terminus, which resulted in a population boom. With the rapid growth, more buildings were constructed, with lumber and coal as the region's primary economic drivers. However, in 1889, a devastating fire leveled many buildings across 116 acres in the city's business district, slowing but not stopping the growth.

Skipping ahead to World War I, the shipbuilding industry became significant to the city, which was the source of 20 percent of the nation's warships. The war also got Seattle national attention for the labor strike enacted over workers' right to maintain the wages they received during the war.

In 1962, Seattle was the host to a genuine world fair, the Century 21 Exposition. The fair led to the construction of the Space Needle and other notable buildings, and in these ways, it continued to leave its mark on the city long after the event was over.

Today, Seattle is a city that embraces change and diversity. Its economy is focused on the tech sector, as opposed to its former days as a center for lumber and coal. It is also a welcoming location for tourism.

Food and Culture

One of the things Seattle is best known for is its association with coffee. The city has the highest rate of coffee consumption in the entire country, and it would be challenging to find another location with a stronger relationship between its residents and their coffeehouses. Additionally, Seattle is the birthplace of mega-chains like Starbucks and Tully's.

When it comes to food, one unique treat that Seattle residents enjoy is the Seattle Dog, which features a hot dog, grilled onions, and cream cheese. This interesting combination is quite a hit with locals.

Given Seattle's placement on the water, it is no surprise that oysters are another top food item. Washington state is known for being the largest oyster-farming state in the country, which means it's always possible to get them fresh in Seattle. While the oysters in particular are exceptional, Seattle is a great destination for all seafood lovers. From the geoduck to the mussels to the sushi, Seattle is in a class by itself when it comes to its seafood options.

Seattle also has a large Vietnamese population, offering access to some of the most amazing pho. It's readily available throughout the city at various locations, making it a staple of Seattle cuisine. There is also plenty of Japanese culture within the city, making teriyaki popular as well. Seattle teriyaki isn't like the traditional recipe and instead uses sugar as a sweetener.

Bars & Nightclubs

For a night on the town, Seattle has many interesting options available. Within Capitol Hill, Pioneer Square, and the University District, there are many bars, brewpubs, lounges, and clubs. While you won't find a club with that heart-pounding bass on every corner, there are enough within the city to make your night a memorable one. From bars with their own art galleries and stunning rooftop views to clubs with full cabarets, Seattle has a truly unique blend of popular locations to give you a night (or even a brunch) to remember.

Unicorn

For a unique experience on the town, you will want to stop in at Unicorn. It's a carnival-themed bar located in the Capitol Hill area. This bar has a premier drag brunch experience called Mimosas Cabaret. For an additional fee, you can enjoy a brunch buffet while you take in the drag performance of a lifetime. The bar also offers interesting weeknight activities like drag bingo, karaoke, trivia night, and variety shows. All their food options are locally sourced and handmade. Additionally, they all have a fantastic carnival theme that brings the show to life.

The kitchen is open every day until 11 p.m., offering you plenty of time to try several options on the menu. Of course, as a bar, they also offer many excellent cocktails. Besides the entertainment, you can take the time to enjoy the photo booth and pinball arcade. This location is one you definitely won't want to skip.

Best Time to Visit: Unicorn is open Monday through Friday from 2:00 p.m. to 1:45 a.m. and weekends from 11:00 a.m. to 1:45 a.m.

Pass/Permit/Fees: The ticket prices for Mimosas Cabaret are $30 each and have a $4.95 service fee when purchased online, which is the recommended option as they sell out quickly.

Physical Address:
Unicorn
1118 E. Pike Street
Seattle, WA 98122

GPS Coordinates: 47.61437° N, 122.31728° W

Did You Know? Unicorn has ranked on several lists of most popular bars, including one that ranks it among the 19 bars you need to drink at before you die.

Rhein Haus Seattle

Once a 1940s candy factory, Rhein Haus Seattle opened its doors in 2013 after being completely renovated. It's like having the world of Bavaria merge with that of the Capitol Hill area. The location is filled with bier hall antiques that make the entire experience as authentic as possible. You'll enjoy genuine Bavarian fare, including homemade sausages and pretzels that are served with 24 different drafts from both European and Northwestern beer collections.

If you enjoy bocce ball, it's another great reason to visit Rhein Haus Seattle. It sports five indoor courts and one outdoor court. There are excellent house rules in place to ensure the game is played fairly. When you make reservations, you have several options, including booking a bocce court with an area for drinks or selecting a table with a personal bocce court. It's known for its casual, classy atmosphere. You'll enjoy a full bar with an excellent DJ for musical entertainment.

Best Time to Visit: Rhein Haus Seattle is open every day from 4:00 p.m. to 2:00 a.m.

Pass/Permit/Fees: To play bocce at Rhein Haus Seattle from Monday through Saturday, the pricing is $10 per person. On Sunday, the rate is $6 per person. For private bocce parties, the rate is $60 per hour.

Physical Address:
Rhein Haus Seattle
912 12th Avenue
Seattle, WA 98122

GPS Coordinates: 47.61165° N, 122.31649° W

Did You Know? Rhein Haus Seattle once operated under the name Von Trapp's.

Q Nightclub

Taking its guests back to the days of superior nightclub experiences, Q Nightclub offers groundbreaking sound, fabulous lighting, and innovative interior design. You'll also find a line of specialty cocktails and drinks, including the club's own line of infused and flavored vodkas. This club offers you multiple options. It's a laidback lounge during the week where you can relax with a drink after work. On the weekend, the Q turns up the volume and raises the beat so that you can dance your heart out. In addition to the spectacular sound, you'll enjoy a superior light show. The combination creates a memorable experience that you won't soon forget.

While the club offers a fun time, be prepared to spend a good bit of money while you're there. Drinks can be a bit on the pricey side. The club features a wide variety of music, including dance and hip-hop, catering to a crowd that wants to get up and move, making Q Nightclub the place to be for a night of dancing.

Best Time to Visit: The Q Nightclub is only open Saturday and Sunday from 10:00 p.m. to 2:00 a.m.

Pass/Permit/Fees: There is a cover charge to enter Q Nightclub that's generally at least $15 and dependent on the event. The prices are subject to change, and tickets are more expensive at the door than they are online. The club offers a coat check for $3 per item.

Physical Address:
Q Nightclub
1426 Broadway
Seattle, WA 98122

GPS Coordinates: 47.61443° N, 122.32026° W

Did You Know? Q Nightclub was at one time an auto garage. It was transformed into the multi-level club of today by designer Bohlin Cywinski Jackson, who is well-known for other projects such as the Apple Cube on Fifth Avenue in New York.

Cha Cha Lounge

Cha Cha Lounge opened its doors in 1998 on Cinco de Mayo alongside the popular local restaurant Bimbo's. The style of the lounge was originally a tiki bar with a ton of Mexican knickknacks. Over the years, it has established itself as a traditional hole-in-the-wall type of location, where guests come to relax amid the old velvet paintings. Throughout its history, what has made the Cha Cha Lounge so special is the use of local musicians as staff. Many local favorites have served food and drinks or checked IDs at the door. Some of the names you may be familiar with have included Modest Mouse, Pretty Girls Make Graves, and the Fleet Foxes.

As business boomed, the lounge and cantina needed a larger site, so they relocated and opened their doors in 2007 at their current location. Instead of being side by side, Bimbo's Cantina is now at street level with Cha Cha Lounge in the basement. The current lounge features a Mexican wrestling motif, but the old velvet paintings remain.

Best Time to Visit: Cha Cha Lounge is open Sunday through Tuesday from 7:00 p.m. to 12:00 a.m. and Wednesday through Saturday from 7:00 p.m. to 2:00 a.m.

Pass/Permit/Fees: There is no cover charge to enter Cha Cha Lounge.

Physical Address:
Cha Cha Lounge
1013 E. Pike Street
Seattle, WA 98122

GPS Coordinates: 47.61470° N, 122.31880° W

Did You Know? Cha Cha Lounge has seen its fair share of celebrity faces over the years. Notable guests have included Drew Barrymore, Britney Spears, Jason Mamoa, Pink, and the Melvins, making this one of the most popular locations to visit in the city.

Deep Dive

As an underwater-themed speakeasy with an entrance hidden within the Amazon Spheres, Deep Dive offers a truly unique experience to all visitors. The decorations are reminiscent of Ariel's hidden collection in *The Little Mermaid*, featuring decaying books, taxidermied animals, and maritime treasures. Deep Dive is fantastically popular, and you should be prepared for a wait that can exceed one hour. However, once you get inside, you'll find it was well worth your patience as you bask in the luxury of the exquisite furnishings.

The food and drinks carry on with the underwater theme, including adding a seafood flare to the famous Seattle Dog by topping it with caviar. All the dining options are tasty morsels, but that's exactly what they are—morsels. Don't come to Deep Dive expecting a gourmet meal, as the offerings are more like appetizers than a main course. If you have something special to celebrate or are looking for an interesting, fun experience, Deep Dive is a lounge you'll want to visit. Note that overly casual attire is not permitted at this location.

Best Time to Visit: Deep Dive is open Sunday through Thursday from 4:00 p.m. to 10:00 p.m. and Thursday through Saturday from 4:00 p.m. to 11:00 p.m.

Pass/Permit/Fees: There is no cover charge to enter Deep Dive.

Physical Address:
Deep Dive
620 Lenora Street
Seattle, WA 98121

GPS Coordinates: 47.61631° N, 122.33942° W

Did You Know? The interior of Deep Dive was designed with Charles Darwin and Jules Verne in mind. The intention was to evoke the curiosity and imagination of the human spirit.

The Crocodile

For all the hottest music, whether it's an up-and-coming local talent or a well-known international phenom, The Crocodile is the scene you want to investigate. This lounge is ideal for offering the best of the best when it comes to live shows. They offer everything from hip hop to punk to folk music. On nights when there are no shows in the main showroom, there are back bar events including bingo, DJ nights, and Tuesday karaoke. This back bar area is also popular among locals for its hot pizza.

The Crocodile recently went through an upgrade, enlarging its floorplan and upscaling the lounge. Despite this being the site of many musical performances, you should be prepared for standing room only. The camera policies vary based on the artist performing, so before you bring one, make sure you check with The Crocodile to ensure you're not violating the rules.

Best Time to Visit: The Crocodile is open every day from 5:00 p.m. to 2:00 a.m.

Pass/Permit/Fees: To attend an event at The Crocodile, you must purchase tickets, which have varying prices depending on the specific event. There is a minimum $2 add-on fee for tickets purchased at the box office. Generally, there is also a cover charge between $15 and $20 to enter the lounge.

Physical Address:
The Crocodile
2505 1st Avenue
Seattle, WA 98121

GPS Coordinates: 47.61546° N, 122.34915° W

Did You Know? Throughout its history, The Crocodile has hosted several world-famous entertainers and bands, including Lizzo, Pearl Jam, Billie Eilish, R.E.M., and Nirvana.

The Hideout

With its unmarked doors, The Hideout can be a challenge to find. Once you're there, it's an easy place to hide away and have a few drinks, just like its name implies. The original plan for the location was to have two separate sections, one for the art and one for the bar, which would support the art operation. However, when owners Greg Lundgren and Jeff Scott finally found the perfect location in 2005, it was smaller than expected and required both aspects of the business to be combined, leading to The Hideout of today.

The service is focused on high-quality cocktails and premium ingredients. You won't find plastic cups or energy drinks in this bar. The artwork truly sets the bar apart from the rest. The Hideout is designed to be a comfortable place where you can feel safe going on your own, which was one of the ultimate goals of the founding duo. What makes this bar even more interesting is that it was founded, developed, and made successful by two individuals with nearly no experience with bar operations.

Best Time to Visit: The Hideout is open every day from 4:00 p.m. to 2:00 a.m.

Pass/Permit/Fees: There is no cover charge to enter The Hideout.

Physical Address:
The Hideout
1005 Boren Avenue
Seattle, WA 98104

GPS Coordinates: 47.61013° N, 122.312569° W

Did You Know? The Hideout was originally started as a five-year performance of sorts with an expiration date; however, it has exceeded that timeframe by over 20 years.

mbar

If you want to take in a stunning view while you enjoy a few cocktails, mbar has everything you're looking for in a bar. It's a rooftop bar located on the 14th floor, offering views of Lake Union, Queen Anne Hill, and North Capitol Hill. This bar is mostly an outdoor location, with only one-third of its accommodations inside the enclosed area of the terrace. Decorated in casual chic and modern styles, you'll feel at home while enjoying a delicious cocktail during happy hour. When it gets chilly outside, mbar has firepit lounge areas to bring back the warmth and keep your evening pleasant.

Don't forget to try the amazing food options while you're there. They include many flavors from around the world with especially heavy Middle Eastern influences. There is a wide selection of drinks, whether you're in the mood for a signature cocktail or a fine wine from an impressive list. High quality and good service come with a price, so expect to wait to get into mbar if you don't have a reservation.

Best Time to Visit: mbar is open Sunday through Thursday from 4:00 p.m. to 9:00 p.m. and Friday and Saturday from 4:00 p.m. to 10:00 p.m. Happy hour is available Sunday through Thursday from 4 p.m. to 6 p.m.

Pass/Permit/Fees: There is no cover charge to enter mbar.

Physical Address:
mbar
400 Fairview Avenue North, 14th Floor
Seattle, WA 98109

GPS Coordinates: 47.62342° N, 122.33417° W

Did You Know? The check-in process at mbar is very unique. The host meets you on the ground floor and leads you to an elevator with no buttons. On the 14th floor, you must travel down a long hallway toward the pulsating music.

The Botanicale

Located in the Fremont neighborhood, The Botanicale is the perfect combination of a secret beer garden and a speakeasy-type tasting room. You can enjoy your beer-tasting experience and then buy some plants. In addition, it's a bit mysterious as it's located down a set of stairs behind a small shop. The best feature of this bar is the drinks it offers. They're not the usual options you'll find in West Coast bars. Instead, they offer a line of unique meads, beers, and ciders. These include things like bocks, sour IPAs, and saisons that come from small-craft producers like Kings and Daughters, Lowercase Brewing, Good Society, and Atwood Farm in Blaine.

The Botanicale is one of the more newly established bars, and it has been met with adoration from all who have visited. So, if you're looking for an interesting but fun way to spend the evening and experience some unique tastes you won't find anywhere else, be sure to stop by this bar.

Best Time to Visit: The Botanicale is open Thursday from 5:00 p.m. to 8:00 p.m., Friday from 5:00 p.m. to 9:00 p.m., Saturday from 1:00 p.m. to 8:00 p.m., and Sunday from 1:00 p.m. to 5:00 p.m.

Pass/Permit/Fees: There is no cover charge to visit The Botanicale.

Physical Address:
The Botanicale
465 N. 36th Street, Suite C
Seattle, WA 98103

GPS Coordinates: 47.65229° N, 122.35288° W

Did You Know? Co-owner Scott Bianchi's goal when establishing The Botanicale was to reach people with all tastes, especially those who expressly claim they don't like one thing or another. He wants to help his guests be open-minded enough to try something at least once, which is where his line of drinks comes into play.

Parks

With over 485 parks to choose from, Seattle provides many ways to stay close to nature. You will have amazing choices between beachfront paths, gorgeous gardens, beautiful forests, and fabulous places to play. These parks are special because they offer the opportunity to escape the hustle and bustle of city life, almost making you forget you're in the heart of one of the country's busiest regions. Despite offering a patch of greenery in an otherwise asphalt world, no two park experiences will be the same, making each one of these locations worthy of the time you spend there.

The Seattle Center

The Seattle Center, first and foremost, recognizes that it is built on the traditional land of the Coastal Salish people. As such, it is a combination of over 30 cultural, sports, entertainment, and educational organizations that produce many public and community programs throughout the year. The Seattle Center features many excellent attractions, including the Chihuly Garden and Glass, Space Needle, Climate Pledge Arena, Bill & Melinda Gates Foundation Discovery Center, Seattle Center Armory, and Seattle Center Skate Plaza.

The Space Needle was constructed in 1962 as part of the World's Fair attractions and has the only revolving glass floor in the world. The Chihuly Garden and Class is an art center that features eight galleries, with a centerpiece of a gorgeous glass house and garden. You'll need as much time as possible here to experience as many attractions as possible. You may even want to plan more than one day. Additionally, while you're in town, you may want to see if there are any festivals occurring since the Seattle Center is home to many excellent events.

Best Time to Visit: The Seattle Center is open daily from 7 a.m. to 9 p.m.

Pass/Permit/Fees: Parking at the Seattle Center starts at $6 per hour. Rates vary based on time and whether there is an event occurring at the park.

Physical Address:
Seattle Center
305 Harrison Street
Seattle, WA 98109

GPS Coordinates: 47.62255° N, 122.35168° W

Did You Know? The Seattle Center is also where the International Fountain is located. This attraction was originally constructed for the 1962 World's Fair and features more than 20 waterspouts that spray. The accompanying selection of music is changed every six months.

T-Mobile Park

If you enjoy baseball, you won't want to miss a trip to T-Mobile Park, the home of the Seattle Mariners. Located in the SoDo neighborhood, this stadium opened its doors in 1999 and is a prominent feature of the Seattle skyline. It's notable for its real grass and massive videoboard, which is the second largest in the league. When you tour the park, you can see all the areas that are generally restricted, including the Owners' Suite, Interview Room, Diamond Club, and many more.

While you're in the stadium, there are plenty of free things to explore. Throughout, you will find various pieces of artwork, including a chandelier made of glass baseball bats and a baseball-themed quilt made of recycled materials. The T-Mobile pen lets you get close and personal with the pitchers as they warm up for a game. There's also the Hall of Fame and Baseball Museum with information and displays where you can learn more about the Mariners and their history.

Best Time to Visit: The best time to visit T-Mobile Park is on game days, which affords you the opportunity to take in a tour and then watch the game.

Pass/Permit/Fees: Tour prices for T-Mobile Park are $15 for adults, $14 for seniors and military, $13 for children 4–14, and free for children 3 and under. Ticket prices for games start at $10 per seat depending on the location in the stadium and the date of purchase.

Physical Address:
T-Mobile Park
1250 1st Avenue South
Seattle, WA 98134

GPS Coordinates: 47.59196° N, 122.33247° W

Did You Know? The nickname for T-Mobile Park is "The House That Griffey Built" in honor of Ken Griffey Jr.

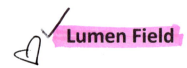 Lumen Field

Over the years, Lumen Field has had many names. It was constructed and opened in 2002 to replace the original Kingdome that was home to both the Seattle Seahawks and Seattle Mariners teams. At that time, both teams were given their own stadiums, allowing them total ownership of their facilities. Lumen Field has a distinctive horseshoe shape and seats for over 68,000 fans. Additionally, it features luxury suites on the north end zone where fans can get a truly up-close-and-personal experience with the game. It has a unique mechanism that causes the reverberation of noise back onto the field at the players, making it a truly challenging experience for opposing teams. When you take in a game or a show at this stadium, you may find yourself torn between the fantastic view of the field and that of the gorgeous Seattle skyline, as both are equally impressive. If football isn't something you enjoy, you can always check the show schedule to see what else the stadium is offering. They have hosted events ranging from boat shows to Beyoncé concerts. Lumen Field also hosts an event called Field to Table where guests can dine on the 50-yard line. Each date features a different local chef and menu. It provides a truly unique experience of the region's food culture.

Best Time to Visit: The best time to visit Lumen Field is during a game or an event. You should check the calendar on the official website to find out when these are happening.

Pass/Permit/Fees: Each event at Lumen Field has a different price. If you are interested in Field to Table, reservations begin at $129 per person. Game tickets start as low as $64 each.

Physical Address:
Lumen Field
800 Occidental Avenue South
Seattle, WA 98134

GPS Coordinates: 47.59579° N, 122.33160° W

Did You Know? Lumen field is the equivalent length of three Boeing 747s lined up end to end.

Beautiful place to walk :)

Gas Works Park

Gas Works Park is unique because it was constructed on the land where the former coal-gasification plant stood. Many of the old plant's former structures still exist, adding character to the park. The city acquired the land in 1965 with the intention of developing it into a park. It wasn't opened for public use for another 10 years. One of the primary features of Gas Works Park is the old boiler house, which has been restructured into a picnic area that features tables and fire grills.

Additionally, the city transformed another plant building into an open-air play barn. The barn is packed with many brightly painted machines for children to interact with. There is also a magnificent hill ideal for kite flying, a sundial, and a fantastic view of the Seattle skyline.

While the park is on the shore of Union Lake, all access to the lake at this point is forbidden. Visitors cannot swim, wade, fish, or boat in the park due to the hazardous conditions of the water, which are a remnant of the park's days as a gas plant.

Best Time to Visit: Gas Works Park is open for day use every day between 6:00 a.m. and 10:00 p.m.

Pass/Permit/Fees: Gas Works Park has no entry or parking fees.

Physical Address:
Gas Works Park
2101 N. Northlake Way
Seattle, WA 98103

GPS Coordinates: 47.64660° N, 122.33427° W

Did You Know? Gas Works Park was once essentially a wasteland that included char bubbling up and oil spills throughout the area. Many considered it a lost cause before it was recovered and made into the park.

Kerry Park

If you're looking for some of the best photographic opportunities during your adventure through Seattle, you must make it a point to visit Kerry Park. It offers exceptional views of the Space Needle and Elliott Bay. On clear days, you can even see all the way to Mt. Rainier. Local photographers are well-acquainted with this park, and you'll likely find them lined up for some of the city's best shots of the skyline. Albert and Katherine Kerry donated the park's land to the city for the purpose of allowing visitors a relaxing place to take in the sights. Kerry's children commissioned a sculpture to add interest to the park in the 1970s.

While your visit to Kerry Park may be short-lived, you will find plenty of other activities and attractions in the area. An ideal visit to the park would be taking in the sunset, seeing the beautiful lights from the city and the boats on the water, and then grabbing an ice cream just a few blocks away at Molly Moon's.

Best Time to Visit: Kerry Park is open for day use every day from 6:00 a.m. to 10:00 p.m. However, sunset is an ideal time to visit as the city begins to light up for an incredible view.

Pass/Permit/Fees: Kerry Park features free entry and parking.

Physical Address:
Kerry Park
211 W. Highland Drive
Seattle, WA 98119

GPS Coordinates: 47.63011° N, 122.35997° W

Did You Know? Kerry Park is touted as offering the best views of the Seattle skyline despite being one of the least-known locations to visitors.

Warren G. Magnuson Park

Located on the shores of Lake Washington, Warren G. Magnuson Park contains 350 acres of land, including pebble beaches, walking trails, sports fields, and picnic spots. In the summer, the swimming area is a favorite spot for its 67-degree water. It also features a lifeguard during peak hours. Guests can also use one of the boat launches, which are separated by motorized and nonmotorized craft.

When you're ready for lunch, there are many picnic areas conveniently placed throughout the park. During the peak season, you'll need to reserve covered sites. The community center features an abundance of indoor activities, including a gymnasium, community garden, and children's basketball courts. There's also a dog park, a windsurfing launch, and a wildlife habitat within the park.

Additionally, this park is where you will find "The Brig," which you'll recognize if you were a fan of *The X-Files* TV show, as it was a common filming location for the series.

Best Time to Visit: Warren G. Magnuson Park is open for day use every day from 4:00 a.m. to 11:30 p.m.

Pass/Permit/Fees: There are no entrance fees for Warren G. Magnuson Park.

Physical Address:
Warren G. Magnuson Park
7400 Sand Point Way NE
Seattle, WA 98115

GPS Coordinates: 47.68195° N, 122.25935° W

Did You Know? Warren G. Magnuson Park was a naval airfield before it was converted into a park.

Green Lake Park

Located in the center of a dense urban neighborhood, Green Lake Park offers visitors an expanse of water and green space. The park was part of the original plan developed by the Olmsted Firm in 1903. However, the state of Washington owned the lake at the time. In 1905, the state gave the lake to Seattle. Today, the park is a preserve for many species of trees, plants, birds, and waterfowl. If you enjoy running or just want to take a long walk, a beautiful 2.8-mile trail extends around the lake.

Green Lake Park is also ideal for swimming and picnics, and there are several access points if you have a boat. It features an expansive playground for the children and a wading pool for the days when the temperature exceeds 70 degrees.

If you're interested in a boating experience, you can stop in at the Green Lake Boathouse and rent a kayak, paddleboat, or canoe. They even have standup paddle boards if you're feeling adventurous. There are also plenty of options for land-based sporting activities, including pickleball, tennis, basketball, and a full golf course that's open seasonally from March to October. Other amenities include a skate park and an off-leash dog park.

Best Time to Visit: Green Lake Park is open all year, 24 hours a day.

Pass/Permit/Fees: Green Lake Park has no entrance fee.

Physical Address:
Green Lake Park
7201 E. Green Lake Drive North
Seattle, WA 98115

GPS Coordinates: 47.68153° N, 122.32868° W

Did You Know? Geologists commonly believe Green Lake and Puget Sound were both formed by the same phenomenon, the Vashon Glacial Sheet.

Olympic Sculpture Park

The Olympic Sculpture Park is owned and operated by the Seattle Art Museum. The museum needed a location to showcase its vast collection of sculptures, so it acquired this nine-acre parkland. The park comprises an outdoor sculpture museum, a beach along Puget Sound, and an indoor pavilion. You'll have the opportunity to enjoy the permanent installations in addition to the changing temporary works. The Seattle Art Museum also includes a rotating selection of artwork from featured artists such as Victoria Haven, Spencer Finch, and Regina Silveira.

As with other reclaimed areas within the city, the Olympic Sculpture Park was once home to an oil and gas company that left behind a wasteland. The Seattle Art Museum made a proposal to recover the land and make it the outstanding sculpture display it is today. There are over 100 sculptures on display. One of the most prominent and well-known sculptures is *The Eagle*, which depicts an eagle taking flight. In addition to the beautiful artwork, visitors can also enjoy breathtaking views of the Olympic Mountains and Puget Sound. While you're out and about exploring, there are plenty of restaurants in the nearby area to make a full day of it.

Best Time to Visit: The Olympic Sculpture Park is open daily, starting 30 minutes before sunrise and ending 30 minutes after sunset.

Pass/Permit/Fees: The Olympic Sculpture Park has no entrance fees.

Physical Address:
Olympic Sculpture Park
2901 Western Avenue
Seattle, WA 98121

GPS Coordinates: 47.61715° N, 122.35545° W

Did You Know? The Olympic Sculpture Park is recognized for being the largest green space in the city of Seattle.

Discovery Park

Discovery Park offers visitors a natural approach to the outdoor experience. There are a few paved trails, but you'll also find many meadows, wooded areas, and a rocky shoreline. You'll have a chance to enjoy excellent views of Puget Sound, the Olympic Mountains, and Mount Rainier, all without having to take an excursion out of the city. Discovery Park offers just over 12 miles of trails, including Discovery Park and Lighthouse Loop Trail, which offer excellent opportunities for birdwatching. Visitors are advised to always remain on the trails because the park has several wildlife-sensitive areas that must be protected.

While you're at the park, you'll likely want to visit the beaches and West Point Lighthouse, which is a favorite among visitors. The park is also home to the Daybreak Star Cultural Center. This center offers educational opportunities that allow guests to learn more about the Indigenous tribes of Seattle through powwows and larger events. Discovery Park was also at one time the site of Fort Lawton. You can still tour the remains of this fort today, viewing the barracks, cemetery, and other military buildings.

Best Time to Visit: Discovery Park is open for day use every day from 4:00 a.m. to 11:30 p.m. The best time to visit is from May to September.

Pass/Permit/Fees: There is no entrance or parking fee to visit Discovery Park.

Physical Address:
Discovery Park
3801 Discovery Park Boulevard
Seattle, WA 98199

GPS Coordinates: 47.66526° N, 122.41233° W

Did You Know? On quiet days, you may be lucky enough to see seals and cranes on the beaches at Discovery Park.

The Klondike Gold Rush National Historic Park

If you're looking for an exciting history lesson on the Gold Rush, then Klondike Gold Rush National Historic Park has everything you need. You can follow the story of the men and women who traveled the path to the Klondike in search of wealth. The park presents itself like a museum and features a full-size replica of a stampeder's cabin, the sleds they used to transport their belongings, and the tools they used to mine for gold. There's also an activity book that children can complete during their visit to receive a Junior Ranger Badge from the National Park Service.

While many staked claims and tried to build their riches through the Gold Rush, most came up empty-handed. The park has a wheel you can spin to test your luck, letting you see if you'd be lucky enough to find gold or go home with nothing. During your visit, you can appreciate the struggle of the miners' journey to reach the Klondike, let alone actually trying to find gold.

Best Time to Visit: The Klondike Gold Rush National Historic Park is open daily, Wednesday through Sunday, from 10:00 a.m. to 5:00 p.m.

Pass/Permit/Fees: There is no entrance or tour fee to visit Klondike Gold Rush National Historic Park.

Physical Address:
The Klondike Gold Rush National Historic Park
319 2nd Avenue South
Seattle, WA 98104

GPS Coordinates: 47.59999° N, 122.33160° W

Did You Know? While the Yukon Territory is the actual home of the gold fields the original stampeders were headed for, Klondike Gold Rush National Historic Park has routes leading in that direction and staging areas to prepare for the trek.

Museums & Galleries

With over 40 museums and galleries to explore, Seattle is a hot spot for cultural and artistic experiences. You'll find everything from traditional dinosaur fossils to cultural icons like Nirvana. The Seattle Center is one of the best locations to start your journey of exploration because of its multiple museums. Capitol Hill and the University District also offer excellent options for museums and galleries.

Chihuly Garden and Glass

Chihuly Garden and Glass is a spectacular showcase of Dale Chihuly's mind-blowing glasswork. There are eight distinct galleries and three Drawing Walls, each of which demonstrates how Chihuly has pushed the boundaries of glass as a medium. The true centerpiece of the location is the Glasshouse. The structure itself is 40 feet tall and made of glass and steel. One of Chihuly's largest suspended sculptures, extending to 100 feet in length, is housed within the building.

The garden also showcases his exceptional glasswork. As you enjoy the beautiful botanical arrangements, you can view the complementary artwork that has been strategically placed throughout. The plants have been carefully selected to accent the art, creating a stunning display. There is also a theater on site where you can view short films that give insight into the glassblowing process, providing a view inside the studio. This theater also hosts many community events and lectures. Visitors can expect to spend a few hours exploring this vast arrangement of artwork to get the full experience of everything it has to offer.

Best Time to Visit: Chihuly Garden and Glass is open every day from 10:00 a.m. to 5:00 p.m.

Pass/Permit/Fees: Admission to Chihuly Garden and Glass is $27 for guests ages 13–64, $24 for King County residents or seniors, $16 for ages 5–12, and free for those 4 and under.

Physical Address:
Chihuly Garden and Glass
305 Harrison Street
Seattle, WA 98109

GPS Coordinates: 47.62117° N, 122.35045° W

Did You Know? The artist behind Chihuly Garden and Glass worked as a commercial fisherman to fund his graduate-school education.

Joey loved it!! *I have been 2-3 times* ☆

The Museum of Flight

As the world's largest independently operated air and space museum, the Museum of Flight has more than 175 different aircraft and spacecraft on display. You'll also find thousands of artifacts, millions of photographs, and several exceptional exhibits that bring out the history of flight. In 1964, the Pacific Northwest Aviation Historical Foundation was created to help preserve the artifacts essential to flight evolution, which were quickly being lost or destroyed at the time.

In 1965, the first Museum of Flight opened at the Seattle Center to display the collected artifacts. In 1975, the first concept for the museum's permanent location began to take shape, with the Port of Seattle offering a 99-year lease on the land that holds the Boeing Red Barn. The Red Barn's restoration was completed in 1983, and it became the first official, permanent home of the museum. Since then, more additions have been added, including the Great Gallery and the Library and Archives Building. The Museum of Flight continues expanding with new exhibits and educational opportunities as often as possible.

Best Time to Visit: The Museum of Flight is open every day from 10:00 a.m. to 5:00 p.m.

Pass/Permit/Fees: The admission prices for the Museum of Flight are $26 for adults, $22 for seniors, $18 for children over 5, and free for children 4 and under.

Physical Address:
The Museum of Flight
9404 E. Marginal Way South
Seattle, WA 98108

GPS Coordinates: 47.51918° N, 122.29673° W

Did You Know? The Caproni Ca.20 was the first fighter plane built worldwide for WWI. The one featured at the Museum of Flight is the only one to have ever been built.

The Museum of History & Industry (MOHAI)

While you're in Seattle, there's no better way to learn about the city and the greater Puget Sound area than by visiting the Museum of History & Industry. This facility features a collection of nearly four million items, including photographs and artifacts. The primary exhibits include the 1919 Boeing B-1, which was Boeing's first commercial aircraft. MOHAI offers permanent and temporary exhibits as well as programming for youths and adults. Its primary exhibit presents a chronological history of Seattle and makes almost a complete ring around the second floor of the museum. This area includes 22 different sections that each feature a different era or event in the city's history.

The Faye G. Allen Grand Atrium takes up the first floor. That's where you will find much of Seattle's cultural history, including the Rainier Brewing Company's historic 12-foot sign and a stuffed cougar donated by Eddie Bauer. The museum's top floor features a small gallery dedicated to the city's nautical history. One of the more recent additions, a gift from Amazon founder Jeff Bezos, was made in 2013. The Bezos Center for Innovation can be found on the first floor in the atrium.

Best Time to Visit: The Museum of History & Industry is open every day from 10:00 a.m. to 5:00 p.m.

Pass/Permit/Fees: Admission prices for the Museum of History & Industry are $22 for adults, $18 for seniors, $17 for students and military, and free for children.

Physical Address:
The Museum of History & Industry
860 Terry Avenue North, Floors 1–4
Seattle, WA 98109

GPS Coordinates: 47.62819° N, 122.33648° W

Did You Know? Of the four million items in the Museum of History & Industry's collection, nearly 100,000 are three-dimensional artifacts and 3.75 million are photographs.

Seattle Art Museum

The Seattle Art Museum features a massive collection of African, American, Asian, Native American, European, and Aboriginal art, among others. The pieces in the collection date from antiquity to the present. In addition to the main collections, the museum features many rotating special exhibits from around the world. The Seattle Art Museum offers many family programs for those of all ages, encouraging a relationship with the arts. Additionally, there are special programs directed at the teen population, engaging the city's youth.

While visiting, you may experience some of the public programs offered by the museum that will make the occasion even more enjoyable, including films and interactive art experiences. They also occasionally feature pop-up performances and outdoor concerts. You can even enjoy a smartphone tour that enlightens you about the history of many of the pieces on display. However, viewing the library collection on site is by appointment only.

Best Time to Visit: The Seattle Art Museum is open Wednesday through Sunday from 10:00 a.m. to 5:00 p.m.

Pass/Permit/Fees: Admission prices for the Seattle Art Museum are $32.99 for adults, $27.99 for seniors and military, $22.99 for students and teens, and free for children 14 and under. There is a $3 discount per ticket if you purchase in advance.

Physical Address:
Seattle Art Museum
1300 1st Avenue
Seattle, WA 98101

GPS Coordinates: 47.61036° N, 122.33813° W

Did You Know? The Seattle Art Museum began with a meager collection of 1,926 pieces in a 25,000-square-foot facility and has since expanded to over 25,000 pieces spread over 312,000 square feet.

Seattle Aquarium

The Seattle Aquarium started in 1977 when the city was the original owner and operator of the facility. In 2010, the Seattle Aquarium Society assumed control over operations. Before that, in 2007, the aquarium added an 18,000-square-foot expansion that included a 120,000-gallon exhibit. Today, the Seattle Aquarium features six major exhibits that will allow you to see many facets of marine life, including the waters of Washington, coral reefs, and shore birds.

You can watch narrated shows where divers interact with fish, experience hands-on activities where you interact with various sea creatures in touch pools, and view many amazing examples of sea life. Daily activities include educational opportunities such as programs on different types of seals, otters, and marine mammals. You'll learn how they live and maybe even catch their feeding times. The Seattle Aquarium also offers guests a café and gift shop to complete the experience.

Best Time to Visit: The Seattle Aquarium is open every day from 9:30 a.m. to 6:00 p.m.

Pass/Permit/Fees: Admission prices for the Seattle Aquarium vary based on the date you purchase. Rates start as low as $29.95 for adults and $20.95 for children. Washington residents receive a discount of $4 and $2.75, respectively. Children 3 and under may visit for free.

Physical Address:
Seattle Aquarium
1483 Alaskan Way, Pier 59
Seattle, WA 98101

GPS Coordinates: 47.60804° N, 122.34296° W

Did You Know? Based on the number of visitors the Seattle Aquarium receives annually, it is the ninth-largest aquarium in the country.

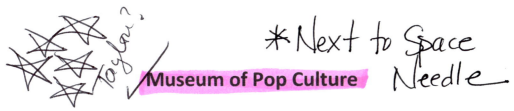

Museum of Pop Culture

Taylor?

*Next to Space Needle

The Museum of Pop Culture offers a unique experience that begins before you ever enter the building. Its façade is designed to resemble a smashed electric guitar made of sheet metal that shimmers in the sunlight. The museum first opened in 2000 as The Experience Music Project, and its primary focus was on Jimi Hendrix, the guitar legend and Seattle native.

However, this initial project wasn't the most successful venture. The Science Fiction Museum was established four years later to add to the visitor experience. In 2011, the museum underwent a massive overhaul, and the Science Fiction Museum was eliminated to accommodate the development and creation of a brand-new science fiction hall of fame. Once construction was complete, the entire venue was rebranded as the EMP Museum. It wasn't until 2016 that the museum finally changed its name it the Museum of Pop Culture, or MoPOP. Today, you can explore a vast collection of exhibits allowing you to experience science fiction and fantasy next to sports and music.

Best Time to Visit: The Museum of Pop Culture is open every day of the week except Wednesday from 10:00 a.m. to 5:00 p.m.

Pass/Permit/Fees: General admission ticket prices for the Museum of Pop Culture vary based on the date and time slot you select. Prices start at $25.25.

Physical Address:
Museum of Pop Culture
325 5th Avenue North
Seattle, WA 98109

GPS Coordinates: 47.62226° N, 122.34821° W

Did You Know? The Museum of Pop Culture was established by Microsoft co-founder Paul Allen.

National Nordic Museum

At the time of its establishment in 1979, the National Nordic Museum was the only North American museum of its kind to represent the five Nordic countries. This museum offers visitors an immersion into Nordic history, including Nordic immigration to the Pacific Northwest. Several exhibits offer an extensive exploration of the pillars of Nordic culture, including displays of art. The museum's primary collection features textiles, artwork, and other pieces brought to the United States through emigration from Nordic countries starting in the 1840s.

In addition to this primary collection, you will find a special Nordic music collection and an exhibit covering the blended history of the Indigenous people of the Seattle region and the Nordic settlers. The museum hosts two major events yearly: Nordic Sól and Julefest. When you visit, you can explore values-based exhibitions and experience programs grounded in Nordic beliefs.

Best Time to Visit: The National Nordic Museum is open Tuesday through Sunday from 10:00 a.m. to 5:00 p.m.

Pass/Permit/Fees: Admission prices for the National Nordic Museum are $20 for adults, $16 for seniors, $15 for college students, $10 for children over 4, and free for children 3 and under. Admission is free on the first Thursday of every month and special exhibits are priced at a reduced rate of $5 per person.

Physical Address:
National Nordic Museum
2655 NW Market Street
Seattle, WA 98107

GPS Coordinates: 47.66908° N, 122.39242° W

Did You Know? Originally, the National Nordic Museum was called the Nordic Heritage Museum. It was housed in the former home of Daniel Webster Elementary School, which closed due to low enrollment.

Pacific Science Center *Next to Space Needle*

The Pacific Science Center was a product of the 1962 World's Fair. It was also founded as the country's first science and technology center. However, very few of the original exhibits remain today. The Pacific Science Center is made of eight buildings containing two IMAX theaters that offer documentaries and feature movies, a laser dome with day and night shows, a butterfly house, and a planetarium that will make you feel like you are in the middle of the galaxy. In addition, you'll find many exhibits to explore.

You'll also have the opportunity to create your own engineering projects, from the design to construction to testing. You can also enjoy the marine touch pool, where you can handle some of the smaller sea life in Seattle. The center features live science shows demonstrating various experiments, and there's even a hands-on exhibit geared toward toddlers. The Pacific Science Center ensures that everyone in your group will find something to enjoy, regardless of their age and interests.

Best Time to Visit: The Pacific Science Center is open Wednesday through Sunday from 10:00 a.m. to 5:00 p.m.

Pass/Permit/Fees: General admission fees for the Pacific Science Center are $27.95 for adults, $25.95 for seniors, and $19.95 for children. Discounts are offered for purchasing advance tickets. IMAX and evening laser dome experiences are an additional fee.

Physical Address:
Pacific Science Center
200 2nd Avenue North
Seattle, WA 98109

GPS Coordinates: 47.62061° N, 122.35145° W

Did You Know? The Pacific Science Center is home to the Pacific Northwest's most prominent laser dome theater.

Seattle Children's Museum

[handwritten: Boys are too big]

The Seattle Children's Museum is the perfect stop for small children who need to stretch their creative muscles. The primary exhibit at the museum is The Mountain, which features a trail that children can follow around. It includes a marmot's den they can hide in and a waterfall they can stand under. There's also an enclosed play area for toddlers at the base of the mountain. Another fun feature is Cog City, where children are introduced to elements of physics by cranking a conveyor belt and dropping balls into chutes.

The Seattle Children's Museum also offers worldly experiences where guests can explore Ghana, Japan, and the Philippines in the Global Village. There are many other real-life experiences for children to explore, including shopping at the market, visiting the optometrist, performing on stage, and exploring a fire truck. In addition, they can also take quiet time in the reading room or create beautiful artwork in the Imagination Studio. Throughout your visit, your child will be encouraged to expand their mind and think outside the box. The museum also has a food court, so you don't even have to leave for lunch.

Best Time to Visit: The Seattle Children's Museum is open Wednesday through Monday from 10:00 a.m. to 5:00 p.m.

Pass/Permit/Fees: Admission for the Seattle Children's Museum is $13 for adults and children, $11 for seniors, and free for those 1 and under.

Physical Address:
Seattle Children's Museum
205 Harrison Street, Floor 1
Seattle, WA 98109

GPS Coordinates: 47.62203° N, 122.35084° W

Did You Know? The Seattle Children's Museum started in 1979 as a single exhibit.

Seattle Asian Art Museum

The Seattle Art Museum was once arranged by artistic influence and had galleries labeled with titles such as China, Japan, etc. The museum was closed for renovations and reimagined to combine all the influences across Asia to tell the story of the human experience. In addition to these 13 thematic galleries, there is a gallery devoted to a special collection that rotates every six months.

The museum began its collection in 1994, focusing on Chinese and Japanese art. Since then, it has grown in variety to include several other influences from across the Asian continent, such as India, the Philippines, and South Korea. After its reopening in 2020, you'll find pieces from Pakistan, China, and India next to one another, which all come together to form one consistent theme.

Best Time to Visit: The Seattle Asian Art Museum is open Friday through Sunday from 10:00 a.m. to 5:00 p.m.

Pass/Permit/Fees: Admission to the Seattle Asian Art Museum is $17.99 for adults, $15.99 for seniors and military, $12.99 for students and teens, and free for children 14 and under. Purchasing your tickets in advance will earn you a $3 discount per ticket.

Physical Address:
Seattle Asian Art Museum
1400 E. Prospect Street, Floors 1 and B1
Seattle, WA 98112

GPS Coordinates: 47.63086° N, 122.31423° W

Did You Know? The Seattle Asian Art Museum is housed the Art Deco building that was once the home of the Seattle Art Museum.

Never Been but sounds fun

Seattle Pinball Museum

You'll find the Seattle Pinball Museum amid the restaurants and markets of the International District where it's been located since its inception in 2010. The museum contains a massive collection of many different types of pinball games spread over two floors.

The best part about this museum is its hands-on design. You can play every single game as often as you'd like during your visit. Games are arranged chronologically, allowing you to see how they progressed over the years. If you find one you particularly enjoy, you're more than welcome to play it several times. Each game features a small placard explaining its history and who created it.

While outside food and drink are not permitted, you can purchase drinks, including draft beer, to enjoy while playing the games. It is important to note that children under 7 are not allowed entry even with a parent.

Best Time to Visit: The Seattle Pinball Museum is open Friday through Monday from 12:00 p.m. to 6:00 p.m.

Pass/Permit/Fees: Admission prices for the Seattle Pinball Museum are $20 for adults and $17 for seniors and children.

Physical Address:
Seattle Pinball Museum
508 Maynard Avenue South
Seattle, WA 98104

GPS Coordinates: 47.59879° N, 122.32500° W

Did You Know? The Seattle Pinball Museum contains playable games from as far back as 1960. The oldest game in the building dates to 1934; however, it is too fragile to be played and is there for educational purposes only.

Burke Museum of Natural History and Culture

The Burke Museum of Natural History and Culture is located on the University of Washington campus, and its curators are the professors. The collections represent a record of the past but are also intended to provide an investment into the future. The collection grows in anticipation of the effects of change, including ecosystem disruption and technological advancements that have yet to happen.

The Burke Museum was originally started in 1879 by a group that called themselves the Young Naturalists. This group met weekly, leading expeditions and holding lectures. By 1885, they had raised enough funds to secure a small building to house their budding collection. Their museum quickly became the hotspot for natural history in the Pacific Northwest. In 1899, the state issued a legislature naming the museum the Washington State Museum. It was again changed in 1962 to honor Judge Thomas Burke, who, along with his wife, was a tireless collector of Native American art. His collection can be seen today in the museum.

Best Time to Visit: The Burke Museum of Natural History and Culture is open Tuesday through Sunday from 10:00 a.m. to 5:00 p.m.

Pass/Permit/Fees: Admission for the Burke Museum of Natural History and Culture is $22 for adults, $20 for seniors, $14 for students and children over 4, and free for children 3 and under.

Physical Address:
Burke Museum of Natural History and Culture
4303 Memorial Way NE
Seattle, WA 98195

GPS Coordinates: 47.66118° N, 122.31154° W

Did You Know? The Burke Museum of Natural History and Culture has grown in size over the years to encompass a collection of 18 million pieces.

Wing Luke Museum

Located within the Chinatown-International District, the Wing Luke Museum ensures its community is at the center of every exhibit it creates. The museum offers authentic stories, perspectives, and experiences from these individuals, allowing guests insight into the meaning of being uniquely Asian. You can see examples from the struggles of early Asian pioneers and view fantastic completed works by Asian American and Native Hawaiian/Pacific Islander (AANHPI) artists.

The facility provides three floors of exhibits for you to explore, including preserved historic areas that you must attend a daily tour to view. The Wing Luke Museum also offers guided tours of the surrounding neighborhood, providing insight into the culture and history of the community. On these tours, guides will point out statues and restaurants that are particularly special to various cultures.

Best Time to Visit: Wing Luke Museum is open Wednesday through Sunday from 10:00 a.m. to 5:00 p.m.

Pass/Permit/Fees: Admission for the Wing Luke Museum of the Asian Pacific American Experience is $17 for adults, $15 for seniors, $12.50 for students, $10 for children 5 and up, and free for children 4 and under.

Physical Address:
Wing Luke Museum of the Asian Pacific American Experience
719 S. King Street
Seattle, WA 98104

GPS Coordinates: 47.59892° N, 122.32291° W

Did You Know? Wing Luke Museum is located in a building that was constructed by Chinese immigrants in 1910.

Henry Art Gallery

Henry Art Gallery first opened in 1927 but wasn't expanded until 70 years later during a major project that quadrupled the size of the facility. This increase was necessary to preserve and exhibit the museum's massive collection, which exceeds 27,500 pieces. The collection includes extensive photography that dates back to the medium's invention and extends to the current period. You can also study the history of printmaking and peruse the vast collection of prints. Other features include textiles, sculptures, and video.

Henry Art Gallery provides a number of public programs to enrich the community. These include screenings, lectures, and public performances. The museum is dedicated to creating an environment of first-hand experiences with living artists, original works of art, and dialogues that encourage discussion of the complex ideas of our time. The museum is known for taking risks with its exhibits. For example, in 1927, it presented the Blue Four, which was regarded as daring at that time. This exhibition marked the first time such works were displayed west of the Mississippi. Following that exhibition, Henry Art Gallery has established and maintained many working relationships with several international artists.

Best Time to Visit: Henry Art Gallery is open Thursday through Sunday from 10:00 a.m. to 7:00 p.m.

Pass/Permit/Fees: General admission to the Henry Art Gallery is free with a suggested donation of up to $20.

Physical Address:
Henry Art Gallery
15th Avenue NE and NE 41st Street
Seattle, WA 98195

GPS Coordinates: 47.65709° N, 122.31168° W

Did You Know? Henry Art Gallery was the first art museum established in Washington.

Famous Buildings & Structures

The architectural style of Seattle is vast and varied across the great city. You'll see elements from the 1900s industrial boom and the rapid growth of technology in the 2000s. You'll find gorgeous, elegantly styled homes in Queen Anne and Pioneer Square neighborhoods and futuristic buildings such as the Space Needle that have an exceptional history.

Over the years, many architects have influenced the development of the city's buildings and structures, including John Graham, Elmer H. Fisher, and Frank Gehry. Seattle's "Northwest Style" has been a constant as many others have come and gone. It has more recently evolved to include green construction and more significant dependence on wood and steel structures.

Space Needle

.he 1962 World's Fair, the Space Needle is one of the ,tructures in Seattle. It offers guests unbelievable views and ⁣ ⁣ ⁣ ⁣ ⁣ ⁣ ⁣ ⁣ ⁣ ⁣ .ce of walking on the world's only rotating glass floor. Its obse⁣ ⁣ ⁣ ⁣ ⁣ ⁣ ⁣ ⁣ .n deck is a mere 520 feet above the ground, offering views of the downtown Seattle skyline and many of the surrounding mountains, including Mount Rainier. The Space Needle's construction resulted from a combination of two designs from well-known architects Edward E. Carlson and John Graham. One design represented a balloon tethered to the ground, and the other displayed a flying saucer. The result was combining the balloon tether's sloping legs with the flying saucer.

While you're at the top of the world, you can also take in a snack or drink at the Atmos Café or Atmos Wine Bar. There is also the Loupe Lounge, which offers an excellent pairing of mixology and gorgeous views. However, the Loupe is restricted to guests 21 and over. While you're visiting, don't forget to take your free welcome picture to commemorate the occasion before stepping out onto the open-air observation deck.

Best Time to Visit: The Space Needle is open daily from 10:00 a.m. to 7:00 p.m.

Pass/Permit/Fees: Admission prices for the Space Needle range from $35–$37.50 for adults, $30–$32 for seniors, and $26–$28 for children.

Physical Address:
Space Needle
400 Broad Street
Seattle, WA 98109

GPS Coordinates: 47.62117° N, 122.34915° W

Did You Know? The Space Needle is specially constructed to withstand hurricane-force winds and earthquakes of up to 9.0 in magnitude.

The Spheres

The Spheres were an endeavor that began in 2013 with a site similar to an indoor garden with many plants and very Mountain Cacao specimen cultivated in 2014 became the first logged in the collection, although the buildings weren't constructed yet. The groundbreaking for construction occurred in 2015, with the steel structure completed in 2016. That same year, the final pane of glass was installed, and its grand opening was held in 2018 after all the plants were installed.

The Spheres features an area called the Living Walls, which has more than 25,000 plants blended together over 4,000 square feet of wall space. The horticulturists who maintain the plants work between The Spheres and an off-site greenhouse in Woodinville. They rotate the plants routinely between the two locations based on the current seasons. When you visit, you will experience cloud-forest species from around the world. It's an opportunity to enjoy the floral displays and learn about the horticulture involved in maintaining these species of plants.

Best Time to Visit: The Spheres has open public hours on the first and third Saturday of each month from 10:00 a.m. to 6:00 p.m.

Pass/Permit/Fees: Admission to The Spheres is free; however, you will need an advance reservation to visit.

Physical Address:
The Spheres
2111 7th Avenue
Seattle, WA 98121

GPS Coordinates: 47.61656° N, 122.33928° W

Did You Know? Despite the name *The Spheres*, the shape of the structure is a pentagonal hexecontahedron and not technically spherical.

Fremont Troll

[handwritten annotation: "...is a fun thing to see. a car"]

At one time, the area beneath the Aurora Bridge in the Fremont neighborhood was an eyesore and a dumping ground for everything people didn't want. In 1989, an art competition was held with the aim of transforming the area. The result was the birth of the Fremont Troll. It was constructed of rebar, cement, and steel. One hand of the giant troll holds a decommissioned Volkswagen Bug that at one time displayed a California license plate until it was vandalized and stolen. Before the vandalism, the car had also held a time capsule full of Elvis Presley memorabilia, but that, too, was stolen. While it is often sprayed with graffiti, it is routinely covered with fresh cement to refresh the exterior.

The Fremont Troll has become a significant fixture in the community and a popular tourist spot. Because the area is busy, you may have trouble finding parking. It's best to park further into the Fremont neighborhood and walk the distance to the Aurora Bridge to visit this famous landmark. Memorabilia items include replicas and Chia Pets. Majungas, a rock band based in Chicago, also created a song titled "The Fremont Troll" in 2016 in honor of the sculpture.

Best Time to Visit: The Fremont Troll is available daily, 24 hours a day.

Pass/Permit/Fees: There is no fee to view the Fremont Troll.

Physical Address:
Fremont Troll
N. 36th Street
Seattle, WA 98103

GPS Coordinates: 47.65164° N, 122.34737° W

Did You Know? The Fremont Troll was originally created as a form of protest against the influence of outsider development.

The Seattle Great Wheel

[handwritten: Never been, Been once :)]

The Seattle Great Wheel had its grand opening in 2012 and features special gondolas with climate control. Most of these gondolas have a maximum capacity of eight passengers. The exception is the luxury cabins that hold four people and feature a glass floor and leather seats. The maximum capacity of the entire wheel is 332 passengers. Seattle was the third North American city to offer this style of wheel to the public, following the ones in Niagara Falls, Canada; and Myrtle Beach, South Carolina. However, of the three, it was the first to be constructed over water, and it extends 40 feet onto Elliott Bay.

The Seattle Great Wheel offers full LED light shows on Friday, Saturday, and Sunday nights. Because of the prime location of the wheel at the iconic Seattle waterfront, you can enjoy a first-class meal following your ride. You can also book a reservation for a four-course meal for four guests while riding on the Seattle Great Wheel. These reservations must be for a standard gondola, as a VIP cabin cannot be reserved.

Best Time to Visit: The Seattle Great Wheel is open Monday through Sunday from 11:00 a.m. to 9:00 p.m.

Pass/Permit/Fees: Ticket prices for the Seattle Great Wheel are $17 for adults, $15 for seniors, $12 for children 4 and up, and free for children 3 and under. Tickets to ride in the Glass Bottom VIP Cabin are $50 per person.

Physical Address:
The Seattle Great Wheel
1301 Alaskan Way
Seattle, WA 98101

GPS Coordinates: 47.60677° N, 122.34252° W

Did You Know? The Seattle Great Wheel is able to provide an amazing light show due to having over 500,000 LED lights.

Suzzallo and Allen Libraries

Considered the most recognizable building on the University of Washington's campus, the Suzzallo Library was named posthumously in honor of Henry Suzzallo, the former president of the University until 1926. The original architects called for three structures to be built in the Collegiate Gothic style and placed in the shape of an equilateral triangular. The first wing that created the western face was completed in 1926, while the southern wing was constructed in 1935. By the time the third wing's construction came around, the university had completely revamped its architectural design to focus on modernist concrete and glass style. In 1990, a fourth wing was added and named the Kenneth S. Allen Library in honor of the father of Paul Allen, Microsoft's co-founder. From 1962 to 1980, Kenneth Allen was the library's associate director. When you visit the Suzzallo and Allen Libraries, the Graduate Reading Room is one of the main rooms you will want to see. It features hand-carved friezes of native plants, stained-glass windows, and painted globes. The Allen wing is well-known for its collection of famous art pieces, and between the two libraries, you'll find over 1.6 million volumes housed there.

Best Time to Visit: The Suzzallo and Allen libraries are open Monday through Thursday from 9:00 a.m. to 8:00 p.m., Friday from 9:00 a.m. to 5:00 p.m., and Sunday from 1:00 p.m. to 8:00 p.m.

Pass/Permit/Fees: There is no fee to visit the Suzzallo and Allen libraries.

Physical Address:
Suzzallo and Allen Libraries
4000 15th Avenue NE
Seattle, WA 98195

GPS Coordinates: 47.65646° N, 122.30780° W

Did You Know? There is a terra cotta bas relief of the original plan for the Suzzallo Library structure that called for a central bell tower to be built located outside the northeast entrance of Smith Hall.

Sky View Observatory at Columbia Center

With its 76 above-ground floors, the Columbia Center is the tallest building in Seattle, making the Sky View Observatory an exceptionally tall public viewing area. The Columbia Center was designed with three concave facades and two setbacks, which lend it the appearance of three buildings in a line. Its base is Rosa Purino Carnelian granite, and the entire building has 8,800 windows. The observatory offers 360-degree views, including the Olympic Mountains, the Seattle Great Wheel, and Puget Sound.

In addition to taking in the views, you can stop by for a light bite to eat at the Sky View Observatory's café. Additionally, if you're looking for a more interesting way to spend a night on the town while exploring Seattle, there is also the option to have a few drinks while you're there. Enjoy an artisanal cocktail while taking in views like no other. It's one of the best places to visit when you get to Seattle, as you can plan the rest of your visit while looking down at the city.

Best Time to Visit: The Sky View Observatory at Columbia Center is open Thursday through Sunday from 12:00 p.m. to 7:00 p.m.

Pass/Permit/Fees: Admission to the Sky View Observatory at Columbia Center is $28 for a standard ticket, $38 for a combination ticket, and $48 for an all-inclusive ticket.

Physical Address:
Sky View Observatory at Columbia Center
700 4th Avenue
Seattle, WA 98104

GPS Coordinates: 47.60509° N, 122.33105° W

Did You Know? There is no taller public viewing area in the Pacific Northwest than the Sky View Observatory at Columbia Center.

Pike Place Market

___ was established in 1907 and was Seattle's first public ___ ially a way for farmers to recoup their costs during a ___ prices were soaring. It encompasses nine acres along ___ waterfront and operates 363 days a year. Pike Place Fish Market ___ always a favorite sight to see. The workers sling the fish from the front to the back to be wrapped behind the counter, earning the name "flying fish."

You can also find many different crafts, as there is a section devoted to 225 local and regional craftspeople with everything from jewelry and fashion to toys on display. Enjoy a fantastic meal at one of the 30 available restaurants, including the famous Athenian Seafood Restaurant and Bar. In addition to the street-level finds, there's another whole world one level down. You can pick up vintage items and collectibles that you won't be able to find anywhere else. Don't forget to stop by Rachel the Piggy Bank for a photo op. Donating some spare change is always welcome, as it funds the Pike Place Market Foundation. This foundation is responsible for a senior center, food bank, and clinic in the downtown Seattle Center.

Best Time to Visit: Although Pike Place Market is accessible all day, the parking garage is only open from 5:00 a.m. to 2:00 a.m.

Pass/Permit/Fees: While admission to Pike Place Market is free, individual services at each business will have their own rates.

Physical Address:
Pike Place Market Parking Garage
1531 Western Avenue
Seattle, WA 98101

GPS Coordinates: 47.60953° N, 122.34180° W

Did You Know? With its long history of operation, Pike Place Market h ___ defined itself as one of the country's longest-operating public ___ ets.

 # The First Starbucks

In 1971, the beginning of a world-famous coffee traditi⟨…⟩ the opening of the first Starbucks. What might be most i⟨…⟩ this debut is that it was operated by a single employee in ⟨…⟩ 1,000-square-foot location. Despite the unassuming store⟨…⟩ you don't immediately see the unique siren logo, you'll identify this coffee shop with no problem. Every day, there's one thing that never changes: the line. Customers, whether locals or Seattle visitors, are constantly stopping in to experience a piece of history at the first Starbucks. The line frequently wraps around the building and down the street, but you'll never wait long as the baristas are first class and keep things moving.

When you visit, you'll see the original building as it was constructed. Nothing has been changed, including the floor, fixtures, and countertops. If you're a Starbucks fan or just love a good cup of coffee, your trip to Seattle won't be complete without stopping in at the first Starbucks while you visit Pike Place Market.

Best Time to Visit: The first Starbucks is open every day from 9:00 a.m. to 4:00 p.m.

Pass/Permit/Fees: There is no admission fee to visit the first Starbucks; however, you will need to pay for your food and drinks, which vary in price.

Physical Address:
Starbucks
102 Pike Street
Seattle, WA 98101

GPS Coordinates: 47.61162° N, 122.34024° W

Did You Know? The inspiration for the name of the first Starbucks came from *Moby Dick*.

King Street Station

King Street Station opened in 1906 and was designed by the same firm that was responsible for New York City's Grand Central Terminal. The building's clock tower was based on Venice's famous bell tower. Inside the station, you'll find stunning architecture, which includes ornamental plaster ceilings, fluted Corinthian columns, terrazzo floors, and wall sconces. The exterior of the King Street Station has remained much the same since its establishment, but the interior has been significantly modified through a series of renovations in the 1940s, 1950s, and 1960s.

Seattle purchased the station in 2008 from the Burlington Northern Santa Fe Railroad Company for $10 to refurbish it. Following the purchase, many significant upgrades were completed during a $50 million renovation, including a terra-cotta roof replacement, repairing the four tower clocks, and completing seismic upgrades. Today, the city is turning the station into an art and cultural hub. While you can use the King Street Station during your stay in Seattle for transportation purposes, it's also a beautiful landmark to visit for viewing a sample of the city's architectural style.

Best Time to Visit: King Street Station is open daily from 6:00 a.m. to 9:30 p.m.

Pass/Permit/Fees: There is no entrance fee to visit King Street Station.

Physical Address:
King Street Station
303 S. Jackson Street
Seattle, WA 98104

GPS Coordinates: 47.59900° N, 122.32991° W

Did You Know? King Street Station hosts over 2.7 million passengers annually.

The Fremont Rocket

Located in the Fremont neighborhood, the Fremont Rocket is a life-size rocket sculpture. It was originally displayed in the Belltown neighborhood until the Fremont Business Association purchased it in 1991 for $750. They had several problems with assembling the rocket and didn't complete the project until 1994. The rocket features the Fremont coat of arms and motto, which embraces each individual's freedom to be peculiar. It is also placed in close proximity to Fremont's Statue of Lenin, which adds to the belief that it is a Cold War relic.

The Fremont Rocket has the standard appearance of a 1920s Art Deco sci-fi space rocket. It even has neon laser pods to function as its ray guns. The rocket also features a launch mode where steam erupts from its base to simulate takeoff. The Fremont Rocket is easy to see when passing through the neighborhood, as no special arrangements are needed to view it. It's one of the quirky landmarks that make Seattle special.

Best Time to Visit: The Fremont Rocket is available to visit daily, 24 hours a day.

Pass/Permit/Fees: There is no entrance fee to view the Fremont Rocket.

Physical Address:
The Fremont Rocket
3420 Evanston Avenue North
Seattle, WA 98103

GPS Coordinates: 47.65131° N, 122.35120° W

Did You Know? Despite being referred to as a rocket fuselage, the Fremont Rocket is not made of genuine rocket parts. Instead, it is composed of parts from a Fairchild C-119 Flying Boxcar.

The Gum Wall

Place Market, there's a regular alleyway that you might ng about. However, when you enter it, you will find the Gum sidered art by many, it was started in the 1990s by local patrons and performers at Unexpected Productions. These individuals stuck their used gum on the wall, beginning a trend that would ultimately lead to a massive wall of chewed gum. Over the years, it has expanded to both sides of the alley.

In 2015, as a preventative measure, all the gum was removed, and the walls were steam cleaned, as the sugar from the gum was eroding them. During this process, 2,350 pounds of gum were removed. However, almost immediately, gum began reappearing. Many contributors to the wall choose to add their gum in artistic patterns instead of just sticking it on the wall. Throughout the year, thousands of visitors stop by for a photo op, including wedding photographs. While in Pike Place Market, take a detour down the alley just south of the market's main entrance. It's a one-of-a-kind artistic experience you won't find anywhere else.

Best Time to Visit: The Gum Wall is accessible all day, every day.

Pass/Permit/Fees: There is no entrance fee to visit the Gum Wall.

Physical Address:
The Gum Wall
1428 Post Alley, Floor 1, Pike Place Market
Seattle, WA 98101

GPS Coordinates: 47.60891° N, 122.34030° W

Did You Know? The Gum Wall was ranked as one of the top five germiest attractions in 2009.

Seattle Center Monorail *Luca's favorite!*

Construction of the Seattle Center Monorail began in 1961, and its public debut was just shy of one month before the start of the 1962 World's Fair. The train's construction cost $3.5 million; however, during the course of the Fair, it carried over 8 million passengers, earning enough income to pay for the costs. After the World's Fair ended, the Seattle Center Monorail was given to Century 21 for free, and in 1965, the corporation sold it for $600,000 to the City of Seattle.

The monorail is made of two trains that each have their own rail. The trains were built in West Germany and then shipped to New York City. They were then transported via a traditional train to Seattle. Each train has a maximum capacity of 450 passengers. The Seattle Center Monorail is the fastest way to travel between the Seattle Center and the downtown area. It's an easy way for you to travel while you're visiting, giving you access to all the amazing attractions at the Seattle Center after your ride on a piece of history.

Best Time to Visit: The Seattle Center Monorail runs daily; however, the operating schedule changes on a daily basis, so you will need to check the website for up-to-date information.

Pass/Permit/Fees: Rides on the Seattle Center Monorail are $3.50 for adults, $1.75 for children and passengers eligible for reduced fares, and free for children under 5. The reduced fare option is for seniors, disabled riders, military personnel, and those with Medicare cards.

Physical Address:
Seattle Center Monorail
370 Thomas Street
Seattle, WA 98109

GPS Coordinates: 47.62412° N, 122.34961° W

Did You Know? The Seattle Center Monorail is a unique public transit system for the state in that the taxpayers do not fund it in any way.

Seattle Public Library, Central Library

The Seattle Public Library was established in the city in 1890. However, it constantly operated from various locations, always needing more space as its collection grew. In 1906, a Central Library Carnegie opened on Fourth Avenue after a fire burned down the library's Yesler Mansion location. Because the library had once again outgrown its home, officials were not very upset about the loss of the mansion. In 1960, the second Central Library opened after it had once again outgrown its original location. That version was upgraded in 1979.

In 1998, Seattle voters approved a bond measure that would double the size of the existing public libraries and build a new Central Library on its current site. The current version of the Central Library is the third installment. It opened to the public in 2004. During construction, the library was moved to a temporary location. Today, it features a four-level "books spiral." In this section, you'll find most of the collection's nonfiction arranged in a continuous loop. There are also dedicated sections for multilingual reading or English as a second language (ESL).

Best Time to Visit: The Central Library is open Monday, Tuesday, Friday, and Saturday from 10:00 a.m. to 6:00 p.m., Wednesday and Thursday from 10:00 a.m. to 8:00 p.m., and Sunday from 12:00 p.m. to 6:00 p.m.

Pass/Permit/Fees: There are no fees to visit the Central Library.

Physical Address:
Seattle Public Library, Central Library
1000 4th Avenue
Seattle, WA 98104

GPS Coordinates: 47.61195° N, 122.33223° W

Did You Know? The Central Library has a capacity of 1.45 million books and materials.

Districts

There have been no official boundaries between neighborhoods in Seattle since 1910. However, districts and neighborhoods have still developed informal lines. These boundaries, and even the names of the districts, have been subject to change throughout the history of Seattle. The city began its initial development during the economic boom driven by the expanding timber industry. During this time, roughly defined neighborhoods sprang up. Local organizations that stimulated civic involvement, such as public libraries and schools, helped further solidify the arrangements. At the turn of the 20th century, community clubs significantly impacted the development of Seattle's neighborhoods, influencing their character and keeping them distinct from others. Since then, further social changes have occurred to help create the districts that are prominent in Seattle today.

Pioneer Square

[handwritten note: Little scary w/ homeless]

Pioneer Square offers visitors many different activities and experiences. There's something for everyone, from history buffs to art lovers. One of your first stops here should be Occidental Square, which features art galleries, indie bookstores, and cafés. It also has a courtyard with a play area for children and one for adults where you can enjoy a giant chess board and game tables.

Another area of interest is the neighborhood's namesake, Pioneer Square. This area is more historically inclined with a totem pole, a bust of Chief Seattle, and historic streetlights. Smith Tower offers an experience to view the Seattle skyline from the observatory and then enjoy drinks during happy hour at the Smith Tower Observatory Bar.

Bill Speidel's Underground Tour will allow you to see the city's appearance before the Great Fire of 1889. Following the fire, the city was rebuilt on top of the remains of the original city. On this tour, you'll have a view of the layer that still exists beneath the surface. When it's time for a meal, there are plenty of dining options, including the Flatstick Pub, Damn the Weather, and Taylor Shellfish Oyster Bar.

Best Time to Visit: The best time to visit Pioneer Square to experience the landmarks and boutiques is throughout the day, while the later hours are best to experience the nightlife.

Pass/Permit/Fees: There is no fee to visit the Pioneer Square neighborhood.

Physical Address:
Pioneer Square, Pioneer Building
101 James Street
Seattle, WA 98104

GPS Coordinates: 47.60255° N, 122.33332° W

Did You Know? The Pioneer Square neighborhood was established in 1852 and is considered the city's original neighborhood.

 Capitol Hill

Capitol Hill is the heart of Seattle's LGBTQ+ life. You'll find rainbow crosswalks and flags that proudly embrace and support all individuals. The nightlife is something to behold in Capitol Hill. It features attractions such as Wildrose, which is one of the last remaining lesbian bars in the United States. Then you can visit Queer/Bar for its glorious drag shows. Liberty is a worker-owned co-op that features coffee, sushi, and craft cocktails. At La Dive, you can enjoy cocktails or natural wine with a side of interesting European fare.

During the day, you can shop to your heart's content. Capitol Hill has everything you can imagine, from brand names to unique boutiques. If you're looking for the perfect makeup, Glossier has just what you need, and Aesop is the ideal shop for finding the best skincare regimen. Ritual and Indian Summer embrace the qualities of Capitol Hill and offer a range of fashion options that celebrate a vast array of gender identities and many sizes, making them true gems in the neighborhood.

Best Time to Visit: Capitol Hill is well-known for its vibrant nightlife and is best visited during the operating hours of these venues.

Pass/Permit/Fees: There are no fees to visit the Capitol Hill district. Individual activities within the community will vary by cost.

Physical Address:
Capitol Hill Station Plaza
918 E. Denny Way
Seattle, WA 98122

GPS Coordinates: 47.61905° N, 122.31998° W

Did You Know? Capitol Hill has long been established as a community of counterculture. In 2020 during the George Floyd protests, the corridor surrounding the Seattle Police Department's East Precinct was barricaded by protesters and established as the Capitol Hill Autonomous Zone.

South Lake Union

[handwritten annotation: "Amazon land"]

The South Lake Union district is named for its proximity to the water. It's located toward the southern end of Lake Union. Because of its prime setting, you'll find many amazing activities on the lake. One unique way to spend some time in the area is by visiting Hot Tub Boats. You'll have the chance to ride in a boat constructed with a full hot tub inside. Lake Union Park is a waterfront park in the district that offers views of the seaplanes taking off and landing right in front of you. The Center for Wooden Boats is a museum located near the lake that offers rentals of their restored boats.

Furthermore, while REI has become a national chain, it has its origins in Seattle. Its original store is still available to visit in South Lake Union. For more shopping options, the seasonal South Lake Union Saturday Market is a must-visit attraction. It runs from May to September and offers a large variety of local food options. You can also stop in at Sub Pop Records, an indie record label. The name might sound unfamiliar at first, but once you hear some of the bands they've produced, it will all make sense. Nirvana and Soundgarden got their start at this label, so stop in to experience a piece of history.

Best Time to Visit: The best time to visit South Lake Union is during the day.

Pass/Permit/Fees: There is no fee to visit the South Lake Union district.

Physical Address:
South Lake Union Saturday Market
139 9th Avenue North
Seattle, WA 98109

GPS Coordinates: 47.61938° N, 122.33988° W

Did You Know? South Lake Union is a hub of innovation that's expanded in recent years to include significant developments in biotechnology.

 Queen Anne

Lower Queen Anne, also known as Uptown, features the Seattle Center. You can visit 11 performance venues and 5 museums in just this one location within the district. Popular attractions include the Seattle Children's Theatre, Memorial Stadium, the Seattle Opera, and the Pacific Science Center. Queen Anne is also located on Lake Union's shores, offering many opportunities for boating and water sports. While you're strolling through the Queen Anne neighborhood, you can even catch a glimpse of the famous house used for exterior shots of Dr. Meredith Grey's house from *Grey's Anatomy*.

Seattle is well-known for its expansive culture of coffee, and Queen Anne won't disappoint. Several local options include the Storyville Coffee Company, Queen Anne Coffee Co, and Millstead. If you're interested in a romantic dinner, be sure to dine at Eden Hill Restaurant. How to Cook a Wolf is another popular restaurant that features Italian-style cuisine. The Queen Anne Beer Hall is an amazing choice for traditional sausages and beer. But Kerry Park is the premier attraction in Upper Queen Anne, as it offers some of the best views of Seattle. For a unique shopping experience, don't forget to stop at Blue Highway Games, a local favorite.

Best Time to Visit: The best time to visit Queen Anne is during the day when most of the attractions are open.

Pass/Permit/Fees: There is no fee to visit the Queen Anne district.

Physical Address:
SW Queen Anne Greenbelt
12th Avenue West to W. Howe Street
Seattle, WA 98119

GPS Coordinates: 47.63153° N, 122.37227° W

Did You Know? Queen Anne has two elevations that feature completely different personalities: Lower Queen Anne and Upper Queen Anne.

Chinatown-International District

The Chinatown-International District is the perfect combination of history and unique experiences. You'll find amazing locations like Maneki, a Japanese restaurant that is over a century old. An alternative is Itsumono, where you can taste delicious options like clams casino on a bed of Korean rice cakes. The city's oldest Chinese restaurant, Tai Tung, is also located within the district.

If you're more interested in fashion, Sairen is a modern boutique that offers clothing from Kenya and Lithuania. You can also purchase locally crafted ceramic mugs here. While you're in the neighborhood, stop at Wing Luke Museum to learn more about Asian cultures. The Chinatown-International District offers a complete array of worldwide treasures, including shopping, dining, and educational experiences.

Best Time to Visit: The best time to visit the Chinatown-International District is during the day when most of the businesses are open. However, timing your visit to match when festivals and events are scheduled is ideal.

Pass/Permit/Fees: There is no fee to visit the Chinatown-International District.

Physical Address:
Seattle Chinatown International
701 8th Avenue South
Seattle, WA 98104

GPS Coordinates: 47.60249° N, 122.32279° W

Did You Know? Despite being called Chinatown-International District, this area does not culturally live up to its name. It started as a predominantly Chinese neighborhood, eventually absorbing Japantown, and continuing to evolve even more over the years to become a cultural hodgepodge.

Ballard

Known for its fine array of dining and shopping options, Ballard has set itself apart from other districts in Seattle. You can find every flavor imaginable within this neighborhood's boundaries. From delectable Thai curries at Pestle Rock to farm-fresh ingredients at Stoneburner, the only problem you'll have is deciding where to start. There is the Anchored Ship Coffee Bar for your coffee fix and Floating Tea Leaves for the tea lovers. Pie Bar and Cupcake Royale are the premier spots for a sweet treat. For a heavier kind of drink, there are plenty of options, including the Ballard Beer Company, Station 18 Drinks & Eats, and Percy's & Co.

Shopping in Ballard offers you the chance to find locally sourced products that aren't available anywhere else. Local retailers in the Ballard neighborhood include Good & Well Supply Co., Ruby Laine Apparel, and the Ballard PCC Community Market. Another shop, Monster, is known for carrying locally crafted home goods and clothing. In addition to the shops and restaurants, Ballard is also home to the National Nordic Museum. The Ballard Locks features a beautiful botanical garden, and Golden Gardens Park offers excellent views of Puget Sound.

Best Time to Visit: The best time to visit Ballard is during the day when the local retailers and restaurants are open.

Pass/Permit/Fees: There is no fee to visit the Ballard neighborhood.

Physical Address:
Ballard Farmers Market
5345 Ballard Avenue NW
Seattle, WA 98107

GPS Coordinates: 47.66796° N, 122.38445° W

Did You Know? Until 1907, Ballard was its own city. At this time, it was annexed by Seattle. It was well-known as the "Shingle Capital of the World."

Belltown

Belltown is recognized as a highly walkable neighborhood where you don't need a lot of transportation options to get you where you want to go. Fifth Avenue is a great spot to grab some interesting eats. At Top Pot, you can snag a donut or head to Eggs and Plants for some falafel. When you're done eating, stop at the Seattle Glassblowing Studio to watch the artists at work.

There are also some classic spots to keep your eye on for the nightlife scene, including The Rendezvous, Ohana, and The Crocodile Café. While you're out at night and need a bite to eat, Belltown Pizza is there to serve. Belltown also has many great dining establishments for full meals such as Umi Saki House and La Fonta Siciliana.

If you're in the market for designer clothes but don't want the designer price tag, there's an amazing consignment shop in the neighborhood called Sell Your Sole Consignment Boutique, which deals in women's wear. In addition to everything Belltown has, it's close to Pike Place Market, Uptown, Downtown, and South Lake Union, making it easy to get from one district to another.

Best Time to Visit: The best time to visit Belltown is during the day for the full experience of the shops and restaurants. However, the nightlife is quite enjoyable too.

Pass/Permit/Fees: There is no fee to visit the Belltown neighborhood.

Physical Address:
Belltown
55 Bell Street Parking
Seattle, WA 98121

GPS Coordinates: 47.61444° N, 122.34813° W

Did You Know? Belltown is known for being the most densely populated neighborhood in the city.

Beaches

When you think of Seattle, beaches are unlikely to be the first thing that comes to mind. However, there is plenty of fun in the sun to be had at the various beaches accessible to the city. From catching some rays to enjoying water sports, the options are vast. Unlike what you may first think of when you hear the word *beach*, the ones in Seattle are a bit different. Many are rocky or pebbly, while others are grassy expanses leading to the water. In addition to enjoying the sun and water, many of the beaches are also part of the local park scene, allowing you to enjoy many other activities during your visit.

Alki Beach

Spend the day in the sun and take in exceptional views of the Olympic Mountains and Puget Sound when visiting Alki Beach. This 2.5-mile beach offers fire pits, volleyball courts, and hand-carry boat access. The volleyball courts are by paid reservation only with the exception of one court that is free for drop-in play. If you're looking for a piece of history, the Log House Museum is near the beach and offers free entry.

Additionally, you won't have to travel far for lunch during your visit, as there are plenty of nearby restaurants.

The beach experiences minus tides, which reveal the vast sandy beach. This summer park destination is partially protected by a seawall. At one time, it was home to an amusement park called Luna Park that operated from 1907 until it was destroyed by a fire in 1931. In 1945, Seattle acquired the site and completed a project to fill it in roughly 9 years later. Alki Beach features a replica of the Statue of Liberty that was given as a gift in 1952. It has become a symbol of liberty and courage to the citizens of Seattle. Many visited the statue to mourn and reflect following the September 11, 2001 terrorist attacks on the United States.

Best Time to Visit: The best time to visit Alki beach is during the summer when the weather and water are warmer.

Pass/Permit/Fees: There is no fee to visit Alki Beach.

Physical Address:
Alki Beach Park
2665 Alki Avenue SW
Seattle, WA 98116

GPS Coordinates: 47.57959° N, 122.40884° W

Did You Know? Alki Beach is the location where the first white settlers of Seattle landed in 1851. There's a monument marking the location.

Mount Baker Beach

Mount Baker Park is a gently sloping ravine that leads to Mount Baker Beach. The beach itself is one of the nicer swimming areas accessible to Seattle; however, the beachfront is not the best choice for sunbathing. Because of this, you will generally find it to be a family-oriented location. For the swimmers, there is a diving board and a swimming raft, and during the summer, there are lifeguards on duty. If you want to try your hand at fishing, there is a fishing pier available. A picnic section is located just above the beach.

Because it is in Mount Baker Park, there are plenty of other activities to participate in. For example, the park has several tennis courts, and there's also a playground. A bathhouse and restroom facilities are available to make the experience much more convenient. Mount Baker Part is also a beautiful location to take in the views of all the different types of trees that grow along the paths, including maples, mountain ash, and chestnuts. Bicycling is popular in the park, and the event known as Bicycle Sunday starts at the northernmost end of the park.

Best Time to Visit: The best time to visit Mount Baker Beach is during the summer when the water and weather are at their warmest.

Pass/Permit/Fees: There is no fee to visit Mount Baker Beach.

Physical Address:
Mount Baker Swim Beach
2521 Lake Park Drive South
Seattle, WA 98144

GPS Coordinates: 47.58366° N, 122.28748° W

Did You Know? Mount Baker Park where the beach is located was part of the original Olmsted plan of 1903 to develop the city's parks.

Madison Park Beach

Madison Park is home to one of the most popular beaches for swimming in Seattle. Madison Park Beach features a nice, grassy area for sunbathing and taking in a beautiful view of Lake Washington. The beach extends 400 feet with cement steps on the northern end and a sandy section on the southern end. While you visit, you can enjoy the diving boards, swimming raft, and children's play area. For everyone's safety, there are also lifeguards employed during the summer. Parking, a bathhouse, and public restrooms are available for your convenience.

The park also features tennis courts, a great play area with baby swings, and updated play equipment. When you're done enjoying the beach, you can step across the street to explore the quaint shops and dine at one of the wonderful restaurants. The Madison Park Co-op community playhouse for toddlers and children is located next to the beach. While you're there, you can take in the views of the floating bridge and the Cascades in the distance. In addition, when you're done at the beach, you'll be just a few minutes away from other locations such as Pike Place Market, Lakebridge Park, and the Seattle Japanese Garden. With everything so close together, you can plan out an entire day of events.

Best Time to Visit: The best time to visit Madison Park Beach is during the summer when the weather and water are warmest.

Pass/Permit/Fees: There is no fee to visit Madison Park Beach.

Physical Address:
Madison Park Beach
1900 43rd Avenue East
Seattle, WA 98112

GPS Coordinates: 47.63625° N, 122.27663° W

Did You Know? Madison Park was the landing location for steamboats from approximately 1890 to 1910.

Seward Park

At 300 acres in size, Seward Park contains one of the last remaining tracts of old-growth forest within the city limits. The park is home to several beaches, miles of hiking trails, an amphitheater, an art studio, and a 2.4-mile path dedicated to walkers and bicyclists. In addition, there are several boat launches. However, motorized boats must have less than 10 horsepower.

In 1911, the land for Seward Park was purchased by the city for $322,000. Its name is a dedication to William H. Seward, the Secretary of State who orchestrated the 1867 purchase of Alaska. In 1917, the meadow leading to the swimming beach was exposed due to the lowering of Lake Washington, making it a highly accessible bathing spot. The bathhouse wasn't constructed until 1927. Then, in 1935, fish-rearing ponds were installed in an effort to make Lake Washington a paradise for anglers. The amphitheater was constructed in 1953 and served as the site of performances led by Gustave Stern for years.

Best Time to Visit: Seward Park is open daily from 6 a.m. to 10 p.m.

Pass/Permit/Fees: There is no entrance fee to visit Seward Park.

Physical Address:
Seward Park
5900 Lake Washington Boulevard South
Seattle, WA 98118

GPS Coordinates: 47.55018° N, 122.25748° W

Did You Know? Seward Park takes up all of Bailey Peninsula, which protrudes into Lake Washington.

Matthews Beach Park

Matthews Beach Park features a wonderful swimming beach where you can cool off in the water. During the summer, they install a diving platform, and lifeguards are on duty. It's also ideal for sunbathing in the grassy area near the water. For those who aren't afraid of the chill, Matthews Beach hosts an annual Polar Bear Plunge on New Year's Day. If going for a swim is not in your plans for the day, you can take your children to the playground, play basketball, or go for a walk on the trail through the park. Matthews Beach also features a hand-carry boat launch if you want to head out in a kayak or canoe. Additionally, the park is located along the Burke–Gilman trail, making it an easy stop if you're exploring the city via the trail.

While you're at Matthews Beach Park, you can enjoy a picnic lunch at one of the designated areas. There are also barbecue pits available. While the area has been inhabited by many peoples since the final glacial period, Matthews Beach Park is named for one individual who set up a homestead in the 1880s: John G. Matthews.

Best Time to Visit: The best time to visit Matthews Beach Park is in the summer when the weather and water are warmest. The park is open daily from 6 a.m. to 10 p.m.

Pass/Permit/Fees: There is no entrance fee to visit Matthews Beach Park.

Physical Address:
Matthews Beach Park
5100 NE 93rd Street
Seattle, WA 98115

GPS Coordinates: 47.69695° N, 122.27410° W

Did You Know? Matthews Beach is known for being Seattle's biggest freshwater swimming beach.

Golden Gardens Park

Golden Gardens Park is a great place to stop if you have your dog with you, as it has an off-leash area at the park's northern end. However, you cannot take your furry friend onto the beach or in the children's play area. The park is located in Ballard along Puget Sound's shores. It offers excellent views of the Olympic Mountains and Puget Sound. In addition to the beach, it features two wetlands and a short loop trail.

While you're visiting Golden Gardens Park, you can walk along the coastline, sunbathe on the beaches, hike forested trails, or fish from a pier. There's also a boat launch if you want to head out onto the water. Six volleyball courts are available as well. Four are by paid reservation only, and the other two are free on a first-come, first-served basis.

Best Time to Visit: Golden Gardens Park is open daily from 4 a.m. to 10 p.m. from the end of May through the beginning of September. All other times, operating hours are from 4 a.m. to 11:30 p.m.

Pass/Permit/Fees: There is no entrance fee to visit Golden Gardens Park.

Physical Address:
Golden Gardens Park
8498 Seaview Place NW
Seattle, WA 98117

GPS Coordinates: 47.69239° N, 122.40305° W

Did You Know? Golden Gardens Park was originally developed in 1907 as an attraction for those who wanted an escape from the city to go to the woods or swim. It was located at the end of the new electric car lines that were being constructed.

Festivals & Annual Events

Seattle is a place full of fun and energy. Because of this, there is almost no end to the festivals and annual events available across the great city. There's something for everyone, from events celebrating various flavors of beer to those surrounding fans' love of comic books. Many festivals and annual events celebrate the multicultural diversity of Seattle. With events geared toward adults and children, the whole family will have something to look forward to. It's important to remember that the events and festivals may change their locations and dates year after year. If you plan your trip around one of these, it is essential to check the schedule and location on their official website.

Bumbershoot Festival

The Bumbershoot Festival is a multidisciplinary arts festival that offers a blend of the best national and worldwide talents. Despite meager publicity, the festival launched in 1971 and was very successful, with over 120,000 attendees. In 1973, the name was changed to Bumbershoot, and the festival continued its steady expansion. In 1980, One Reel, a local production company, took over the festival's management. The festival saw decades of expansion, including the addition of flavors of the flavors of Seattle.

Eventually, in 2019, One Reel's partner AEG declined to renew its contract for the festival. Then, in 2020, all public concerts were canceled due to the COVID-19 pandemic. Unfortunately, due to unforeseen circumstances, the festival has been on a hiatus since then. With a new manager announced, the plan is to have a bigger and better experience in 2023, kicking off a new history of the Bumbershoot Festival for all to experience.

Best Time to Visit: The Bumbershoot Festival is held annually during Labor Day weekend.

Pass/Permit/Fees: Ticket prices for the Bumbershoot Festival vary based on the package you purchase. Prices for the festival are released closer to the time of the event, often with early bird deals.

Physical Address:
Seattle Center
305 Harrison Street
Seattle, WA 98109

GPS Coordinates: 47.62258° N, 122.35159° W

Did You Know? Bumbershoot is a term that means "umbrella." Its selection for the Bumbershoot Festival was intended for two reasons. First, it acknowledges Seattle's rainy weather. Second, the festival is intended to be an umbrella for all aspects of the arts.

Seafair Festival

The first Seafair Festival was held in 1951 to celebrate the city's centennial anniversary. In 1966, the U.S. Navy Blue Angels joined the festivities and performed an air show at each festival. Every summer, the Seafair Festival kickoff occurs when the Seafair Pirates land at Alki Beach in mid-June. This group changes leadership each year but performs several acts of charity throughout the city in addition to the shows. The Torchlight Parade started as a small affair at the initial Seafair Festival. Over the decades, it has grown to be one of the largest parades in the country.

Seafair Weekend is the festival's highlight and features parachute acts from the U.S. Army Golden Knights, the Seafair Log Boom, and the Boeing Seafair Air Show. Additionally, this is the part of the festival where the Blue Angels perform their synchronized flight pattern. In addition to all the air shows, you can easily find yourself at a block party celebrating the occasion.

Best Time to Visit: The Seafair Festival is a summer-long event that begins in mid-June. However, the most exciting part of the festival occurs Friday through Sunday during the first weekend in August.

Pass/Permit/Fees: General admission to the Seafair Festival for a single day is $35 per person. Prices are subject to change each year.

Physical Address:
Seafair Foundation
2101 4th Avenue
Seattle, WA 98121

GPS Coordinates: 47.61489° N, 122.34272° W

Did You Know? Until the 1960s, it was part of the tradition of the Seafair Festival to burn a ship in Puget Sound.

Folklife Festival

The Folklife Festival is held annually, rain or shine. You'll want to be prepared no matter what the weather forecast calls for. It's long been the herald of summer's beginning for the residents of Seattle. The festival is a collection of traditional, folk, and ethnic arts and music. The event was first held in 1972 and is now the largest of its kind in the country. You'll see many local acts that perform across the 20 stages placed throughout the Seattle Center. Several buskers come to perform along the walkways, including jugglers, musicians, and magicians.

While you're at the festival, you can explore the different vendors that offer everything from arts and crafts to clothing. Performances include drum circles, poetry readings, and dancing in the fountain. The Folklife Festival partners with the Circle of Indigenous Peoples to bring educational opportunities to those attending the festival. During the celebration, traditional arts and cultures of the region are showcased, and it's an amazing opportunity to learn about Indigenous traditions. While the festival is free to enter, you will want to bring money for food and souvenirs.

Best Time to Visit: The Folklife Festival is held annually over Memorial Day weekend.

Pass/Permit/Fees: Admission to the Folklife Festival has historically been free.

Physical Address:
Seattle Center
305 Harrison Street
Seattle, WA 98109

GPS Coordinates: 47.62261° N, 122.35168° W

Did You Know? The Folklife Festival spotlights a specific ethnic community or folk tradition each year, bringing about cultural awareness.

Día de Muertos Festival Seattle

Día de Muertos is a celebration of the dead and their impact in our lives. It's not meant to be a day for mourning. On this day, people honor their loved ones with gifts of food, music, and dance. They behave as if they were there beside them. The goal is to welcome the spirit of the deceased into the home.

The Día de Muertos Festival seeks to bring this tradition to the people of Seattle and its visitors. The festival offers face painting, elaborate altars, many performances, visual art, workshops on creating sugar skulls, and many other excellent activities. The history of the festival dates back to 1998 when a group of volunteers met to plan a Day of the Dead celebration in South Park. The event steadily expanded from Concord Elementary School to other venues within that area until it finally moved to its home at the Seattle Center in 2003.

Día de Muertos has changed throughout the centuries from the original celebration of Indigenous peoples to take on influences by the Spanish, resulting in the celebration we know today. It's an exciting opportunity to experience cultural differences in celebrating life and death. If you're in town when this festival kicks off, be sure to stop in and enjoy some of the entertainment and activities.

Best Time to Visit: The Día de Muertos Festival Seattle is held annually toward the end of October.

Pass/Permit/Fees: Admission to Día de Muertos Festival Seattle is free for everyone.

Physical Address:
Seattle Center
305 Harrison Street
Seattle, WA 98109

GPS Coordinates: 47.62255° N, 122.35172° W

Did You Know? Historians believe Día de Muertos could date back 2,000 years to various civilizations such as the Aztecs and Toltecs.

Emerald City Comic Con

Emerald City Comic Con is the destination for all things geeky in the Pacific Northwest. It provides guests with the best that the comic and pop-culture industries offer straight from the hands of the producers. From quality content to fabulous guests, fans have the experience of a lifetime at this festival. The Emerald City Comic Con features guests across many industries, including anime, comics, literature, and entertainment. With many well-known names in each area, guests can meet their favorites and get autographs.

It's also a great opportunity to dress up. No Comic Con would be done right without a healthy dose of cosplay, especially the ECCC. There's even a full competition to see who has the best costume. So, if dressing like your favorite character is on your agenda, make sure you bring your best costume and join in the fun. You can also attend workshops to learn tips and tricks to expand your knowledge of creating costumes and being the most authentic version of your favorite characters. The Emerald City Comic Con also hosts a charity art auction to raise money for research at St. Jude's Children's Hospital. If you're interested in buying a piece of art, you'll be funding an excellent cause.

Best Time to Visit: Emerald City Comic Con is held the first weekend in March.

Pass/Permit/Fees: General admission tickets to the Emerald City Comic Con start at $40 for adults. You can also purchase 4-day passes for $140. Children's 4-day passes are $25.

Physical Address:
Seattle Convention Center, Arch Building
705 Pike Street
Seattle, WA 98101

GPS Coordinates: 47.61242° N, 122.33147° W

Did You Know? Attendance for the Emerald City Comic Con reached over 75,000 over a 4-day period in 2022.

Lunar New Year Fair

Wing Luke Museum is the perfect place to host the Lunar New Year Fair in the Chinatown-International District. It begins with an outdoor event called the Lion Dance, which is said to bring good luck into the new year. It involves a group dressed in a large lion dancing to music in the street. Because the dance involves loud noises and firecrackers, the museum offers ear protection for those who are sensitive to sounds. This dance represents traditional Asian Lunar New Year activities, giving you an authentic experience without traveling to another country. Once the Lion Dance is over, the festivities move inside the museum, where guests can participate in crafts, games, and viewing a special Lunar New Year exhibit.

Additionally, the museum has open access to all its galleries, allowing you to learn about amazing AANHPI individuals. You can take your time exploring the regular exhibits, or you can participate in the activities the museum has arranged for the day. There are also events where you can learn ceramics and calligraphy. Wing Luke Museum has packed a vast array of experiences into the five hours that make up the Lunar New Year Fair, making it a memorable experience for everyone.

Best Time to Visit: The Lunar New Year Fair generally takes place around the last weekend of January or the first weekend of February.

Pass/Permit/Fees: Outdoor events at the Lunar New Year Fair are free to attend. Indoor events have admission fees of $17 for adults and $10 for children.

Physical Address:
Wing Luke Museum
719 S. King Street
Seattle, WA 98104

GPS Coordinates: 47.59897° N, 122.32287° W

Did You Know? The Lunar New Year Fair offers raffles geared toward children ages 12 and under.

The Seattle International Film Festival

The Seattle International Film Festival features several hundred films that guests can view in various Seattle locations. At the heart of the festival is a competition across several categories to decide which films are the best in their class. The primary features are independent and foreign films; however, many viewers also come for the documentaries.

The Seattle International Film Festival debuted in 1976 and quickly gained popularity. Without the monumental influence of the festival, Dutch films wouldn't have impacted the U.S. film industry as they did. There's also a Secret Festival containing four films guests have no information about before viewing. In addition, they have to sign an agreement not to share what they have viewed. If you're interested in new or unorthodox film selections, the Seattle International Film Festival may have exactly what you're looking for. They feature everything from family-friendly options to culturally important films from around the world.

Best Time to Visit: The Seattle International Film Festival is held annually in May and June.

Pass/Permit/Fees: Packages and tickets for the Seattle International Film Festival start at $75 and cap at $2,500 depending on the services you wish to purchase.

Physical Address:
Seattle Center
305 Harrison Street
Seattle, WA 98109

GPS Coordinates: 47.62258° N, 122.35164° W

Did You Know? The Seattle International Film Festival has evolved into a hybrid experience. Half of it will be in person at theaters throughout the city, while the other half will be held virtually.

Seattle Latin Dance Festival

If you enjoy getting up and dancing to your heart's content, attending the Seattle Latin Dance Festival is a must. They offer workshops and a boot camp where you can learn all the hottest moves from professionals in Latin dance. The trainers teach social dancing and focus on all the skills you'll need on the dance floor. After each lesson, you'll have the confidence to go out on the floor and mix it up with like-minded individuals from around the world.

At night, sit back and watch the fantastic performances of the greatest talents with all their sultry moves and lively music. You can get up on the dance floor at the Social Dance and interact with friends and new acquaintances. The underlying purpose of the event is to bring together dancers from around the world to enjoy their love of dance together.

Best Time to Visit: The Seattle Latin Dance Festival is held annually in October.

Pass/Permit/Fees: Guest passes for the Seattle Latin Dance Festival start at $50. A boot camp option for intensive training must be combined with a guest pass for an additional $60.

Physical Address:
Hilton Seattle Airport & Conference Center
17620 International Boulevard
SeaTac, WA 98188

GPS Coordinates: 47.46493° N, 122.29266° W

Did You Know? The Seattle Latin Dance Festival features talent from around the world, including dancers from Poland.

The Seattle Improv Festival

The Seattle Improv Festival brings together individual improvisers from around the world. They spend the week participating in workshops with masters in the field. At the end of the week, several performances showcase the talents they developed throughout the workshops. Over the years, the festival has seen many great teaching masters, including Sheila Daniels, Lisa Kron, Charna Halpern, and Avery Schreiber. Each year, the festival takes a special theme. Past themes have included Old Friends, Blurred Lines, The Fool, Zen, and Trinity: The Rule of Three.

The Seattle Improv Festival is hosted by Unexpected Productions, a local company that produces shows year round and hosts classes. The first Seattle Improv Festival was held in 1997, and it generally falls around the anniversary of the founding of Unexpected Productions. Attending the festival is a great way to watch some fantastic improvisational acting. It's a completely different experience from viewing a well-scripted and rehearsed theatrical performance.

Best Time to Visit: The Seattle Improv Festival is held annually at the end of June.

Pass/Permit/Fees: A festival pass for the Seattle Improv Festival is $30.

Physical Address:
Seattle Festival of Improv Theater
5510 University Way NE
Seattle, WA 98105

GPS Coordinates: 47.66951° N, 122.31290° W

Did You Know? Unexpected Productions is the result of three different improv groups joining together. They called themselves The Seattle Theatresports League. Additionally, this was the first U.S. group to perform Theatresports.

Indigenous People Festival

Seattle is a city built on the traditional lands of the Coastal Salish people, which is a fact acknowledged by most businesses upfront on their websites and other public-facing information. Because of this, there is a tight bond with the Indigenous peoples of the area. The Seattle Center Festál added the Indigenous People Festival to its roster to celebrate Indigenous cultures and bring them to the rest of the world.

At this festival, you can experience songs, dances, food, and knowledge from those who have come to spread their culture with guests. The Seattle Indigenous Health Board is a co-sponsor of the festival. It's well-known for its specialization in caring for Indigenous people. Their healthcare processes are rooted in Indigenous practices for a holistic approach to treatment, ensuring mind, spirit, and body are all equally cared for. The event offers many excellent activities, including film screenings. In addition, you can watch live performances. Performers have included Blue Heron Canoe Family and White Hawk Family. The tribes also have vendors who sell art, jewelry, and clothing. Some of the proceeds go back into the Seattle Indigenous Health Board, so you know you'll be contributing to a good cause.

Best Time to Visit: The Indigenous People Festival is held annually in June.

Pass/Permit/Fees: The Indigenous People Festival offers free admission to everyone.

Physical Address:
Seattle Center
305 Harrison Street
Seattle, WA 98109

GPS Coordinates: 47.62218° N, 122.35088° W

Did You Know? Seven out of every ten Native Americans now live in an urban area.

Festival Sundiata Black Arts Fest

Festival Sundiata Black Arts Fest is named for the Sundiata Keita. He was the legendary Mansa of West Africa's Mali Empire. He was responsible for rescuing his people's Griot and creating one of the most culturally significant kingdoms on the continent. The festival was created to celebrate art and educate the community about people of African descent. It includes music, spoken word, art exhibitions, food, vendors, and much more.

However, the shining achievement of Festival Sundiata Black Arts Fest is its ability to unite families and diverse communities through its activities. There is also a reception where you can meet with the artists who have their work on display at the festival. Hearing their stories will add more depth to their art. You'll also have the opportunity to purchase any pieces you absolutely love. With over 40 years of experience bringing the history and culture of people of African descent to the Pacific Northwest, Festiva Sundiata Black Arts Fest works to bridge the gap across cultures.

Best Time to Visit: Festival Sundiata Black Arts Fest is held annually in July.

Pass/Permit/Fees: Festival Sundiata Black Arts Fest does not charge an admission fee.

Physical Address:
Seattle Center
305 Harrison Street
Seattle, WA 98109

GPS Coordinates: 47.62218° N, 122.35088° W

Did You Know? The first Festival Sundiata was held in 1980, making it the longest-running festival focusing on the culture and history of people of African descent in the Pacific Northwest.

Seattle Queer Film Festival

The Seattle Queer Film Festival has become a central fixture in the Seattle queer film community. During the festival, the films are eligible to receive awards that are decided on by a panel of jurors. Three Dollar Bill Cinema produces the Seattle Queer Film Festival. Their primary mission is to provide the community with exceptional films about LGBTQIA+ individuals.

At the festival, filmmakers have the chance to interact with their audiences and other filmmakers. The event takes place across Seattle at more than one cinema. Past venues have included the AMC Pacific Place, Northwest Film Forum, and SIFF Cinema Egyptian. You may even find yourself at an after party following one of the fabulous showings at these local hotspots. More recently, the Seattle Queer Film Festival has evolved into a hybrid affair, allowing guests to attend both in person and virtually. There are also fantastic parties, community meetups, filmmaker panels, and educational workshops. On any day that you can attend this festival, there's something exciting to do.

Best Time to Visit: The Seattle Queer Film Festival is held annually in October.

Pass/Permit/Fees: Admission to the Seattle Queer Film Festival ranges from $13–$30.

Physical Address:
Three Dollar Bill Cinema
1122 E. Pike Street #1313
Seattle, WA 98122

GPS Coordinates: 47.61401° N, 122.32461° W

Did You Know? Established in 1996, the Seattle Queer Film Festival is the largest festival of its kind in the Pacific Northwest.

Northwest Flower & Garden Show

The Northwest Flower & Garden Show offers a fantastic viewing experience for those who can't get enough of the blooms. Garden designers from across the Pacific Northwest come together to create a beautiful display for all to enjoy. There's even a section on the Skybridge that offers excellent ideas for those living in city apartments to incorporate plants into their interior design.

In addition, there's an abundance of marketplace options. You'll find many different kinds of gifts available for all the people in your life and possibly even the perfect plant to add to your collection. Throughout the event, there are many free seminars where you can learn helpful tips on raising your plants and creating your own garden, whether it's full size or in a container. Each year, there's also a children's treasure hunt in the main gardens. They can pick up a treasure hunt form and complete it for a chance to win a prize. For the adults, there's a Blooms and Bubbles event where you can sip on champagne while designing your own floral creation to take home.

Best Time to Visit: The Northwest Flower & Garden Show is held annually in February.

Pass/Permit/Fees: Tickets to the Northwest Flower & Garden Show are $21 for early bird adult purchases, $26 for same-day adult purchases, $12 for students, $38 for a 2-day pass, $80 for a 5-day pass, and $13 for a half-day pass. Opening night party tickets start at $250 per person.

Physical Address:
Seattle Convention Center, Arch Building
705 Pike Street
Seattle, WA

GPS Coordinates: 47.69239° N, 122.40305° W

Did You Know? The spectacular gardens at the Northwest Flower & Garden Show are constructed in under 72 hours each year.

Children's Film Festival

The Children's Film Festival is operated by the Northwest Film Forum, which selects international children's films from many countries. This festival celebrates the best and brightest in the international film industry directed specifically toward children. The roster includes animation, short films, feature films, and even some hands-on workshops. Its overarching goal is to inspire the younger generation to participate in their local and global communities as agents of change.

The Children's Film Festival of Seattle greatly emphasizes visual storytelling with a central focus on the childhood experience. Their primary priority is sharing stories that the mainstream media has underrepresented. These stories also provide inspiration for viewers to have empathy and a better understanding of the world around them.

Best Time to Visit: The Children's Film Festival is held annually in February.

Pass/Permit/Fees: Passes for the Children's Film Festival range from $90–$190. In-person tickets cost $7–$14, while virtual tickets are $5–$25.

Physical Address:
Northwest Film Forum
1515 12th Avenue
Seattle, WA 98122

GPS Coordinates: 47.61507° N, 122.31698° W

Did You Know? The Children's Film Festival has become the largest event of its kind in the western part of the country.

The Seattle International Auto Show

The Seattle International Auto Show is a car lover's dream come true. Featuring more than 300 vehicles of the highest caliber, including vintage and new models, you'll have your fill of the finest cars on the West Coast. Popular brands that have been featured are Rolls Royce, Lamborghini, and Bentley. In recent years, the event has included a larger showcase of electric vehicles, as more environmentally conscious consumers lean toward this type of car. A great example was the 2022 return of Hummer to the festival with their new Hummer EV Truck.

Many vehicles on display at the Seattle International Auto Show aren't even available yet, giving you the opportunity to glimpse the newest advancements in the industry and what's coming. There's also a Then & Now display that pairs vintage cars along with their newer models so that you can see the difference time has made. The show even has a section dedicated to children with face painting and other family-centered activities that will keep them entertained.

Best Time to Visit: The Seattle International Auto Show is held annually in November.

Pass/Permit/Fees: Tickets to the Seattle International Auto Show are $17 for adults, $15 for seniors and military, and free for children 12 and under. VIP tours are $35 per person.

Physical Address:
Lumen Field Event Center
800 Occidental Avenue South
Seattle, WA 98134

GPS Coordinates: 47.59403° N, 122.33222° W

Did You Know? The Seattle International Auto Show features iconic vehicles like the BMW 1969 E3S and many others.

Zoos & Animals

Seattle is home to some of the most amazing zoos with fantastic options for viewing the world's wildlife. Some of these amazing locations provide excellent rehabilitation services for endangered animals, preventing their extinction. In general, visiting the zoo is a great way to break up a long trip with something fun and exciting for the entire family to do together. Everyone will learn something new and get to experience different animals and habitats they may never see anywhere else. Seattle zoos have a fantastic reputation and are known for being vocal about preserving endangered species and balance in the natural world.

Washington State Ferries

State Ferries are a government-owned and operated ... serve pedestrians and drivers in the Puget Sound and ... areas. With 21 vessels, it's the largest fleet in the ... original plan of Washington State was to operate the ferry system until bridges were built across Puget Sound. However, the bridges were never built, leaving the ferries as a necessity.

The fleet's largest vessels can carry a maximum of 202 vehicles, and their passenger limit is 2,500 people. Washington State Ferries plans to electrify the fleet to make it more sustainable by reducing carbon emissions. At one time, the fleet also operated passenger-only vessels but ended those routes and sold the vessels to other operators. While visiting Seattle, you can cross Puget Sound with Washington State Ferries as a passenger or with your vehicle. If you've never been on a ferry before, it's an experience you won't want to miss.

Best Time to Visit: Washington State Ferries operate daily. However, schedules vary between routes, and visitors should review schedules ahead of time on the official website.

Pass/Permit/Fees: Fares for Washington State Ferries start at $13.55 for a car and driver.

Physical Address:
Washington State Ferries
2901 3rd Avenue #500
Seattle, WA 98121

GPS Coordinates: 47.62055° N, 122.35184° W

Did You Know? Washington State Ferries originated as part of the mosquito fleet, which was a collection of small steamer lines that once served Puget Sound toward the tail end of the 19th century and early part of the 20th century.

Woodland Park Zoo

The Woodland Park Zoo was established in 1899 and spans 92 acres. It's currently home to more than 900 animals and 250 distinct species. Some of these species are endangered and in the zoo to be protected and preserved. You'll experience everything from the African Savanna to the seasonal Molbak's Butterfly Garden when you visit. The zoo has many amazing animals, including lions, hippos, penguins, tigers, and gorillas.

In addition to the amazing animals present in the Woodland Park Zoo, there is also the gorgeous Woodland Park Rose Garden. Since 2006, they have not used any pesticides in the garden, allowing them to feed spent flowers to the animals in the zoo. Within this garden, you can see almost 3,000 roses that cover more than 200 varieties.

Best Time to Visit: Woodland Park Zoo is open Monday through Wednesday from 9:30 a.m. to 4:00 p.m. and Thursday through Sunday from 9:30 a.m. to 3:00 p.m.

Pass/Permit/Fees: General admission tickets to the Woodland Park Zoo are $19 for adults, $17 for seniors, $13 for children, $16 for military personnel, and $10 for children of military personnel. Disabled guests receive a $2 discount. Parking is $6 for the first two hours, then $2 for each hour after.

Physical Address:
Woodland Park Zoo
5500 Phinney Avenue North
Seattle, WA 98103

GPS Coordinates: 47.66898° N, 122.35088° W

Did You Know? In 1975, the Woodland Park Zoo established immersive habits that recreated the original habitats of the animals as closely as possible, setting a standard that many other zoos soon followed.

Debbie Dolittle's Animal Encounters

Debbie Dolittle's Animal Encounters is a hands-on experience for interacting with many different animals you would never find in your everyday experience. These include kangaroos, armadillos, and capybaras. While not every animal will consent to be touched—the armadillo is a tricky one—you are welcome to make friends with every one you meet. There is also the option to visit Otter Park and have a one-on-one encounter with otters or sloths.

When you book your appointment, you'll choose which encounter you're interested in. The trained guides will help you through the experience to ensure you know how to make the most of it. You'll also receive feeding buckets as part of your entrance fee. In addition to the otters or sloths, you'll have the chance to tour the other animals available at the park, including wallabies and coatimundi.

Best Time to Visit: Debbie Dolittle's Animal Experience is open Friday through Sunday from 11:00 a.m. to 6:00 p.m.

Pass/Permit/Fees: Admission to Debbie Dolittle's Animal Experience is $13 per person and free for children 2 and under. Animal Encounters can be booked for $89 per person with a 2-person minimum.

Physical Address:
Debbie Doolittle's Animal Encounters
120 138th Street South, Suite B
Tacoma, WA 98444

GPS Coordinates: 47.13301° N, 122.43255° W

Did You Know? When visiting the petting zoo at Debbie Dolittle's Animal Encounters, you can upgrade your tickets to visit the farm where the larger animals go once they no longer fit in the petting zoo.

Theaters

It was December of 1894 in Pioneer Square when Thomas Edison's kinetoscope was displayed to the citizens of Seattle. Not long after that, projection technology advanced and the city began its love affair with film. Movie theaters began appearing all across the city, drawing large crowds. In the 1960s and 1970s, several of the older Seattle buildings were repurposed into movie theaters. This passion extended through the arts to the opera and live theatre, with other buildings devoted to these art forms. Today, there are still many great theaters across the city of Seattle that are beloved by residents and visitors alike.

Seattle Opera

The Seattle Opera was incorporated in 1963, and its very first performances were of Puccini's *Tosca*. The company has been historically recognized for its many excellent performances of Richard Wagner's work. For example, in 1975, it was the first U.S. company since 1939 to perform the entire *Ring* cycle over the course of a week. The Seattle Opera performed the *Ring* cycle for the last time in August of 2013 and has stated that there are no plans for future productions.

The company is well-known for bringing important stories to life on its stage. One of its more recent premieres was based on Khaled Hosseini's *A Thousand Splendid Suns*, based on the critically important novel that has captivated millions. With internationally acclaimed singers, you'll be drawn into the tales they sing, whether it's a modern story or an age-old favorite from Wagner. Today, the company produces its shows in a new state-of-the-art auditorium resulting from a multimillion-dollar upgrade project. Whether it's your first time attending the opera or you're a diehard fan, the Seattle Opera is an experience you'll want to add to your visit to the Emerald City.

Best Time to Visit: The Seattle Opera is open Monday through Friday from 10:00 a.m. to 6:00 p.m.

Pass/Permit/Fees: Performance tickets for the Seattle Opera start at $35 per person.

Physical Address:
Seattle Opera
563 Mercer Street
Seattle, WA 98109

GPS Coordinates: 47.62507° N, 122.34966° W

Did You Know? The Civic Auditorium at Seattle's Civic Center was renovated and established as the original Seattle Opera House in 1962.

Seattle Rep

Seattle Rep is one of the country's most renowned regional theatres, producing various classics, new works, and Broadway hits. The company is unafraid to produce edgy shows that get to the heart of social matters. Many famous actors have graced the stages, including Lawrence Fishburne, Samuel L. Jackson, Christopher Walken, and Meryl Streep. Additionally, many Seattle artists have built a home at the theatre. These local actors include names like Suzanne Bouchard and R. Hamilton Wright. Seattle Rep has also premiered plays by famous playwrights Neil Simon, August Wilson, Sarah Ruhl, and many others.

The theatre features a program called Project Yes, which fosters budding artists to help bring them into their careers. When you attend a production at Seattle Rep, you could be experiencing history in the making as a new artist marks the start of achieving their dreams. The theatre also sponsors a program called Bringing Theatre into the Classroom that enables K–12 teachers to incorporate theatre into their curricula, providing more student enrichment.

Best Time to Visit: Seattle Rep is open Tuesday through Friday from noon to 5 p.m. for in-person ticket sales. Showtimes will vary by show, which you can verify on your tickets.

Pass/Permit/Fees: Tickets to Seattle Rep start at $22 per person.

Physical Address:
Seattle Rep
155 Mercer Street
Seattle, WA 98109

GPS Coordinates: 47.62461° N, 122.35357° W

Did You Know? Seattle Rep's first home was the Seattle Playhouse, which was built as part of the World's Fair in 1962.

Seattle Children's Theatre

Officially founded in 1975, the Seattle Children's Theatre initially faced financial struggles in 1983. Then, under new leadership in 1984, things drastically turned around for the better, with the theatre becoming the country's second-largest performing arts center dedicated to children. Within a few years, the theatre outgrew its original home and needed an upgrade. In 1993, the Charlotte Martin Theatre opened at the Seattle Center, offering guests much more space than the original location. A little less than two years later, a second venue opened adjacent to the first at the Eve Alford Theatre.

The Seattle Children's Theatre is internationally recognized for its theatre productions, educational programs, and new scripts geared toward youth. The theatre has an extensive history of productions, including many that were world premieres. Today, you can enjoy productions at either location, with every show specially produced just for children and their families.

Best Time to Visit: The Seattle Children's Theatre is open Monday through Friday from 9:00 a.m. to 5:00 p.m.

Pass/Permit/Fees: Admission to the Seattle Children's Theatre starts at $20.

Physical Address:
Seattle Children's Theatre
201 Thomas Street
Seattle, WA 98109

GPS Coordinates: 47.62108° N, 122.35220° W

Did You Know? The technical start of the Seattle Children's Theatre was in 1971 with the formation of the Poncho Theatre, which was located on the grounds of what was then called Woodland Park Children's Zoo.

The Seattle Public Theater

The Seattle Public Theater is a small facility that can accommodate 165 guests per show. It's housed in the historic Bathhouse Theatre. The building was originally established as an actual public bathhouse in 1927. While the productions at one time mainly centered on late 19th-century and early 20th-century theories, the company has since expanded to incorporate major conversations that resonate locally and globally.

The theater has made it a mission to become a venue that speaks life into the moment. They strive to create a community of inclusion that sparks the engagement of ideas and people. When you take in a production at the Seattle Public Theater, you'll clearly see their efforts in action through art that celebrates women and diverse identities.

Best Time to Visit: The Seattle Public Theater lobby opens one hour before showtime, which will change based on your selected show. Verify showtimes on your tickets.

Pass/Permit/Fees: Standard admission tickets to The Seattle Public Theater are $36.

Physical Address:
Seattle Public Theater
7312 West Green Lake Drive North
Seattle, WA 98103

GPS Coordinates: 47.68275° N, 122.33984° W

Did You Know? The Seattle Public Theater aims to make theater accessible to all and, through this venture, has a program that can make tickets affordable for everyone, whether it's in their budget to attend the theater or not. Through this method, the theater aims to increase inclusion for all.

Seattle Symphony

The Seattle Symphony held its first performance in December 1903. Since then, it has established its unique place in the symphonic music world. Sir Thomas Beecham was responsible for developing the orchestra's skill and reputation during the formative years. The Seattle Symphony's educational programs were greatly expanded during the 22-year tenure of Milton Katims as music director. The orchestra went on to have its first European tour in 1980. In the following decades, the orchestra continued its development of excellence, earning several awards and nominations. Today, the Seattle Symphony seeks to unleash the power of music by bringing people together and lifting the human spirit. They offer a program called Tiny Tots to introduce the family's youngest members to music through songs and games, making the experience educational and fun. The next level of programming is called First Concerts, which is geared toward those who are 3–5 years old. In this series, musicians play short pieces and encourage questions from young audience members. When you plan your visit, you can choose the type of show that's best suited to you and your family, whether you want to experience a full orchestral production or a special program.

Best Time to Visit: The best time to arrive at the Seattle Symphony is 20 to 30 minutes before your chosen show starts. Times will vary by show and should be verified on your tickets.

Pass/Permit/Fees: Admission to the Seattle Symphony starts at $30 per person.

Physical Address:
Seattle Symphony
200 University Street
Seattle, WA 98101

GPS Coordinates: 47.61370° N, 122.33616° W

Did You Know? The orchestra at the Seattle Symphony has won five Grammy awards and two Emmy awards.

Other Fun Attractions

In addition to the main attractions in Seattle, like the famous buildings and beaches, there are plenty of fun activities and locations you'll want to visit. These attractions range from the strange to the exciting and will broaden your view of the Emerald City. From touring old Seattle beneath the streets to visiting the graves of famous icons, there's a little something for everyone in and around the city. As you plan your trip, don't forget some of these excellent locations to round out your experience. You won't regret it!

Bruce Lee and Brandon Lee Grave Sites

The Bruce Lee and Brandon Lee grave sites are located in Lake View Cemetery, which is next to Volunteer Park in the Capitol Hill district. More than just two graves, this spot has become a global pilgrimage site. Because of the massive influx of visitors daily, shrubs had to be planted around the graves to protect the neighboring sites from damage. Those coming to pay their respects leave little trinkets and flowers for the father and son.

Many find a deep connection in visiting the sites because of Bruce Lee's personal history of overcoming adversity. As an immigrant, martial artist, and actor, he was a major influence in many sectors. People from many backgrounds and cultures feel a close connection to his personal struggle to achieve success. Additionally, when people think of martial arts, Bruce Lee is often the first name that comes to mind. The cemetery staff asks that anyone visiting be mindful of other visitors, especially if there is a service occurring. When you visit, it's unlikely for there to be any large crowds, but you should expect to see a steady stream of visitors.

Best Time to Visit: The Bruce Lee and Brandon Lee grave sites are open to the public every day between 10:00 a.m. and 4:00 p.m.

Pass/Permit/Fees: There is no entrance fee to visit the Bruce Lee and Brandon Lee grave sites.

Physical Address:
Bruce Lee and Brandon Lee Grave Sites
1554 15th Avenue East
Seattle, WA 98112

GPS Coordinates: 47.63394° N, 122.31584° W

Did You Know? Bruce Lee was 32 years old when he passed away, and despite there being more than 50 years since his passing, cemetery staff say there's never a day that goes by without a visitor at his grave.

Jimi Hendrix Grave

World-famous rock musician and renowned guitarist Jimi Hendrix died on September 18, 1970. He was laid to rest in a simple grave in the same cemetery as his mother. Despite the simplicity of the gravestone, his devoted fans flocked to it to pay their respects for years.

Decades after Hendrix's death, his father, Al, finally realized a deep-seated desire to honor his son with a memorial that did justice to his memory. In 2002, he had his son's remains reburied underneath a stone gazebo built over the previous years. This memorial consists of a dome supported by three pillars. You'll find a portrait of Hendrix etched in stone within the monument. His original headstone is also inside.

The family plot now surrounds the monument, and a sundial has been placed with it. When you enter the Greenwood Memorial Park cemetery from Monroe Avenue NE, you'll find the memorial on the roundabout directly in front of you. While the Jimi Hendrix Grave is just outside Seattle, it's worth the extra distance to experience a piece of musical history.

Best Time to Visit: Greenwood Memorial Park is open 24 hours a day, year round. However, the best time to visit is from spring through fall when there is no snow.

Pass/Permit/Fees: Visiting the Jimi Hendrix grave site is free.

Physical Address:
Greenwood Memorial Park & Funeral Home
350 Monroe Ave NE
Renton, WA 98056

GPS Coordinates: 47.48828° N, 122.17433° W

Did You Know? It's estimated that more than 14,000 Jimi Hendrix fans visit the grave each year, which is what prompted the upgrade to the current monument.

Boys will love it

GameWorks Seattle

If you love to game, you have to make a stop at the premier gaming destination in the city: GameWorks Seattle. This spot has over 150 eSports games and features a lounge for competitive play. It has PlayStations, Xboxes, and gaming PCs for every type of game you could want to play. There is also a full arcade with classic and cutting-edge titles. In addition, they have added virtual reality booths. You won't even have to worry about finding dinner because they have a kitchen on site for dining options.

GameWorks is a leader in the competitive and casual gaming experience, ensuring your visit will be absolutely memorable. To make things easier for everyone playing in the arcade, the machines aren't operated by quarters. Instead, they have an easy system where you purchase your credits to play. You'll easily recognize GameWorks Seattle when you get close by, as the entrance is decorated with gaming art featuring iconic characters.

Best Time to Visit: GameWorks Seattle is open Wednesday from 12:00 p.m. to 8:00 p.m., Thursday from 12:00 p.m. to 9:00 p.m., Friday from 12:00 p.m. to 10:00 p.m., Saturday from 11:00 a.m. to 10:00 p.m., and Sunday from 11:00 a.m. to 8:00 p.m.

Pass/Permit/Fees: GameWorks Seattle does not charge admission unless there is a special event. Playing games costs $22 for 120 credits, $27 for 190 credits, $37 for 260 credits, and $52 for 400 credits.

Physical Address:
GameWorks Seattle
1511 7th Avenue
Seattle, WA 98101

GPS Coordinates: 47.61191° N, 122.33385° W

Did You Know? GameWorks Seattle was first developed as a creative venture by mega corporations DreamWorks, Sega, and Universal Studios.

Haunted History Ghost Tours of Seattle

For a fun way to explore the historical side of the city with a haunted twist, you'll want to try Haunted History Ghost Tours of Seattle. Since 2017, they've been rated as one of the city's best tours. The company states that all tour guides are paranormal investigators or psychics, not actors playing roles. All stories shared have been collected from the owners' three decades of living in Seattle. They have compiled evidence and history from locals, legends, and visitors and evaluated it for authenticity before sharing it with their guests.

The tour is a walking one that involves stairs. It will take you to dark, cramped places. All participants must be a minimum of 16 years old. If you're interested in adding some excitement and interest to your vacation, make sure to book one of the Haunted History Ghost Tours of Seattle to learn more about the city's darker side. The owners promise a very authentic experience that you won't soon forget.

Best Time to Visit: Haunted History Ghost Tours of Seattle is open Thursday through Saturday from 2:00 p.m. to 10:00 p.m.

Pass/Permit/Fees: Tickets for Haunted History Ghost Tours of Seattle are $15 per person.

Physical Address:
Haunted History Ghost Tours of Seattle
508 2nd Avenue
Seattle, WA 98104

GPS Coordinates: 47.60215° N, 122.33184° W

Did You Know? Haunted History Ghost Tours of Seattle is owned and operated by professional paranormal investigative experts with experience in occult studies.

Burke–Gilman Trail

The Burke–Gilman Trail stretches almost 19 miles from Seattle to Bothell. It functions as a thoroughfare for those commuting to work just as much as it is an essential site for social recreation and fitness. The trail was constructed in the 1970s and was among the first rail trails, inspiring many similar projects throughout the country. The boundaries of the Burke–Gilman Trail are marked by Golden Gardens Park and the Sammamish River Trail.

In 1885, Thomas Burke and Daniel Gilman, two well-known Seattle residents, established the Seattle, Lake Shore, and Eastern Railway. The railway was then purchased by the Northern Pacific Railroad in 1901. The line was sustained by heavy traffic from the logging industry through 1963; however, the corridor later became inactive in 1971. Today, trail users travel from Puget Sound to Lakes Union and Washington. While walking along the trail, you'll pass through the Fremont neighborhood, where you can glimpse the famous Fremont Rocket and Fremont Troll. Many also take the opportunity to bike along the trail. There is a section where the trail between Ballard and the University of Washington is missing. However, if you want to return to nature while visiting Seattle, the Burke–Gilman Trail is the perfect opportunity.

Best Time to Visit: The best time to hike the Burke–Gilman Trail is between spring and fall when there is no snow.

Pass/Permit/Fees: There is no fee to hike the Burke–Gilman Trail.

Physical Address:
Blyth Park
16950 W. Riverside Drive
Bothell, WA 98011

GPS Coordinates: 47.75069° N, 122.20895° W

Did You Know? The Burke–Gilman Trail was instrumental in developing the concept of "rails to trails."

I have done a tour - interesting

Ballard Locks Fish Ladder

At Ballard Locks Fish Ladder, you can see the amazing journey salmon take as they journey upriver toward their freshwater spawning grounds. The salmon must acclimate themselves from saltwater to freshwater, so they remain within the area of the locks for around six hours or more, giving visitors ample time to view them through the windows. You'll see the largest species among these salmon, the King Chinook Salmon.

The U.S. Army Corps of Engineers constructed Ballard Locks Fish Ladder and opened it in 1917. It aims to act as a gateway between Puget Sound and the upstream lakes. You can view the opening of the locks and the boats lifting from one body of water to the next. In addition to watching the salmon and seeing the boats pass through the locks, you can visit the Ballard Locks botanical garden. In the summer, you can even enjoy musical performances among the flowers. So, even if the salmon aren't very active when you arrive, there are plenty of things for you to see and do at Ballard Locks Fish Ladder.

Best Time to Visit: Fish can be viewed at Ballard Locks Fish Ladder from late spring through early fall.

Pass/Permit/Fees: There is no fee to visit the Ballard Locks Fish Ladder.

Physical Address:
Ballard Locks Fish Ladder
2930 W. Commodore Way
Seattle, WA 98199

GPS Coordinates: 47.66486° N, 122.39756° W

Did You Know? You can see three species of salmon at Ballard Locks Fish Ladder: Chinook, Sockeye, and Coho.

The Seattle Waterfront

The Seattle Waterfront is an open-air promenade that will keep you busy all day long with something to offer everyone in your group. At one end of the boardwalk, you'll find the amazing Seattle Aquarium. Choose your lunch from beloved establishments such as Ivar's Fish Bar, Premier Meat Pies, and The Frankfurter.

After lunch, make your way to The Seattle Great Wheel for a spectacular view of Puget Sound and the Seattle skyline. Be sure to stop in at Ye Olde Curiosity Shop and have a look at their interesting wares. They have all the oddities you can think of, including shrunken heads. Take the time to explore each pier, as they all have something different to offer, from the shops to the food. They're also within walking distance of landmarks like Pike Place Market and Olympic Sculpture Park.

These central historic piers are home to the busiest ferry fleet in the country as well as the cruise ferries that travel to Alaska. The Seattle Waterfront is also an excellent place to find public art. There are sculptures, fountains, murals, and more that you can explore for free. You'll need the whole day to enjoy everything the waterfront has to offer.

Best Time to Visit: The Seattle Waterfront is open every day from 7 a.m. to 9 p.m.

Pass/Permit/Fees: There is no entrance fee to visit the Seattle Waterfront.

Physical Address:
Republic Parking
9 Wall Street
Seattle, WA 98121

GPS Coordinates: 47.61319° N, 122.35060° W

Did You Know? The whale-watching boat, the *Victoria Clipper*, operates from Pier 69.

Seattle Chocolate

When you first start your factory tour at Seattle Chocolate, you'll be invited into a tasting room to sample some delectable melted chocolate. You'll also be treated to a film that teaches you where the cacao beans are sourced from, how they're harvested, and the process that's used to make them into delicious chocolates. After the video, visitors can enter the factory. Cell phones and other items are not permitted onto the factory floor, and lockers are provided for safekeeping.

Many of the chocolates made at Seattle Chocolate are created by hand, not a machine. You'll have the chance to watch all of this in motion as long as they are in production that day. After the factory tour, you'll head back to the tasting room for more samples. What you get to taste is a surprise, but it will allow you to decide what you want to buy when you head to the chocolate shop. After the enjoyable experience of watching how the sweets are made and getting a taste, you'll likely want to purchase some to take with you. The shop will have plenty to offer.

Best Time to Visit: Seattle Chocolate is open Monday through Friday from 10:00 a.m. to 6:00 p.m. and on Saturday from 10:00 a.m. to 5:00 p.m. However, production occurs Monday through Thursday, so those are the best days to plan your trip.

Pass/Permit/Fees: Ticket prices for the factory tour at Seattle Chocolate are $12 for adults and $10 for children.

Physical Address:
Seattle Chocolate
1180 Andover Park West
Seattle, WA 98188

GPS Coordinates: 47.44347° N, 122.325367° W

Did You Know? Seattle Chocolate focuses on sustainability and is part of the Rainforest Alliance. In addition, they give back to the local community to help feed those in need.

Interesting

Bill Speidel's Underground Tour

You're in for a great adventure when you sign up for Bill Speidel's Underground Tour. If you recall back to your high school history class, the Great Fire of 1889 severely damaged the city. Instead of demolishing the remains, Seattle built on top of it. This tour will take you down below the city you know today to view what existed over 100 years ago. It starts beneath Doc Maynard's Public house, moves into Pioneer Square, then heads beneath the city.

The tour guides will entertain you with hilarious tales, keeping the entire journey lighthearted and fun. You'll finish up in the Underground Gift Shop, where you can pick up a souvenir to remember the occasion. The shop carries *Sons of the Profits*, which was written by Bill Speidel and serves as the basis of the tour. Doc Maynard's is an excellent choice to grab a quick snack before the tour starts, or make a plan to get a full meal after it's over. There's even a combination ticket that allows you to have lunch with your tour.

Best Time to Visit: Bill Speidel's Underground Tour is open every day from 9:30 a.m. to 7:00 p.m.

Pass/Permit/Fees: Ticket prices for Bill Speidel's Underground Tour are $22 for adults, $20 for seniors and students, $10 for children, and $50 for a combination ticket for the Underground Tour and Paranormal Experience.

Physical Address:
Bill Speidel's Underground Tour
614 1st Avenue
Seattle, WA 98104

GPS Coordinates: 47.60250° N, 122.33370° W

Did You Know? Bill Speidel mounted a campaign with other residents to get the city to make Pioneer Square a historic district to preserve the country's largest collection of Victorian-Romanesque structures. His Underground Tour was the result of his efforts.

The Seattle Japanese Garden

The Seattle Japanese Garden was opened to the public in 1960 and has become one of the most highly regarded North American Japanese-style gardens. Gardening in Japan is considered an art form, and this garden was styled under that guiding principle. It covers three and a half acres and adheres to a style known as stroll gardens, which was developed in the late 16th to early 17th century. This type of garden follows a winding path around a central pond, inviting guests to experience the different landscapes of Japan.

Juki Iida, the renowned landscape artist, combined traditional Japanese plants with local flora to create the garden. Since the establishment of the garden, these plants have gently spread across the land, forming the display you see today. With each passing season, the Seattle Japanese Garden slowly reveals new colors and fragrances that make it an amazing experience you will enjoy.

Best Time to Visit: The Seattle Japanese Garden has variable hours every Tuesday through Sunday at different times of the year. It typically opens at 10 a.m. and closes anywhere from 4 p.m. to 7 p.m. based on the season. It's closed from July 11 through August 8 and from December through February.

Pass/Permit/Fees: Admission to the Seattle Japanese Garden is $10 for adults; $6 for seniors, students, military personnel, and children over 5; and free for children 4 and under.

Physical Address:
Seattle Japanese Garden
1075 Lake Washington Boulevard East
Seattle, WA 98112

GPS Coordinates: 47.62917° N, 122.29628° W

Did You Know? The Seattle Japanese Garden is one of four specialty gardens in the city.

The University of Washington Campus

One of the most beautiful sections of the University of Washington campus is the quad. It's home to 30 Yoshino cherry trees that offer immense beauty when they're in full bloom. They're known for attracting visitors from around the world. Meanwhile, Red Square is the hub of campus life. You'll find everything from information booths to food trucks there. The university also has botanic gardens that you can visit. They include Japanese gardens and six other areas. You can even explore them by canoe. The Suzzallo Library is also located on campus. This library boasts amazing architecture in addition to its massive collection of materials. You'll see a bronze W at the entrance from 45th Street and 17th Avenue NE. It's an ideal photo opportunity, as many of the students take selfies when they pass by. While you're there, you should snap a quick photo to commemorate the occasion. For more photo opportunities, Drumheller Fountain is set in front of a perfect view of Mount Rainer. It's the perfect spot to photograph the mountain and capture the beautiful fountain simultaneously. It's ranked as one of the best views you'll find on campus.

Best Time to Visit: One of the best times to visit the University of Washington campus is in the third week of March, as this is when the Yoshino cherry trees are in bloom.

Pass/Permit/Fees: There is no admission fee to visit or tour the University of Washington campus.

Physical Address:
Visitors Center
4060 George Washington Lane Northeast
Seattle, WA 98195

GPS Coordinates: 47.65685° N, 122.31071° W

Did You Know? The University of Washington Campus is the site of many famous inventions, including vinyl, bubblegum, and synthetic rubber.

Seattle Shakespeare Company

The Seattle Shakespeare Company holds the plays of William Shakespeare and other class playwrights at a high level of regard, considering their works to be timeless while still crossing social and cultural boundaries. For them, these plays explore the vast expanse of the human experience. They firmly believe these works contain insights that are relevant to contemporary audiences, sparking their desire to produce first-rate productions of these classics.

A group of local theatre artists established the company in 1991 and have since evolved it into the state's only year-round classical theatre company. Depending on which show you attend, you may experience the true classical version or an updated twist on an old favorite. For example, the company modified *The Taming of the Shrew* to take place in a trailer park setting in more recent times. With their creative practices and provocative performances, you can experience Shakespeare's works in a whole new light.

Best Time to Visit: The Seattle Shakespeare Company's hours vary by show. You can verify your showtime on your tickets.

Pass/Permit/Fees: Ticket prices for the Seattle Shakespeare Company vary depending on the show you select. A limited number of shows begin at $10.

Physical Address:
Seattle Shakespeare Company
305 W. Harrison Street, Floor 1
Seattle, WA 98109

GPS Coordinates: 47.62162° N, 122.35091° W

Did You Know? The Seattle Shakespeare Company offers a variety of programming, including free outdoor productions, to ensure that everyone has the opportunity to attend the theatre regardless of socioeconomic status.

Seattle Wine Tours

You'll want to try Seattle Wine Tours if you enjoy flavorful wine. The best part is you won't have to worry about returning to your hotel after you've sampled a few vintages because they drive you to and from the wineries. You can select the locations you want to visit or let the experts at Seattle Wine Tours customize a tour just for you. Your chauffeur will drive you through the city to each destination while providing you with the history of important landmarks you pass.

During your tour, you'll be escorted to two or more award-winning wineries, depending on what you want from the experience. Seattle Wine Tours has a unique relationship with the winemakers, so if you'd like to meet them, it's possible. They can even set it up for you to have a taste straight from the wine barrel. In addition, you'll be riding in style, as the fleet of vehicles the operation owns are all high class and offer the utmost comfort. While you may have been on a wine tour before, you've likely never experienced anything like this. You can sit back, relax, and enjoy Seattle's best wines while being driven through the city like a celebrity. It's a first-class experience you won't want to miss out on.

Best Time to Visit: The best time to enjoy Seattle Wine Tours is on a day when your desired winery is open for tasting.

Pass/Permit/Fees: Rates start at $93 per hour for Seattle Wine Tours and depend on which vehicle you choose from their fleet. Tours can be anywhere from four hours to multiple days.

Physical Address:
Seattle Wine Tours
4660 E. Marginal Way South
Seattle, WA 98134

GPS Coordinates: 47.56142° N, 122.33904° W

Did You Know? Seattle Wine Tours will make your adventure fun and easy by picking you up wherever you are staying.

Pacific Northwest Ballet

The Pacific Northwest Ballet was established in 1972. In its early stages, it was a component of the Seattle Opera. In 1977, the two organizations separated from one another, and the ballet took its current name a year later. Since then, it's become one of the country's largest and most highly respected ballet companies. The company is comprised of almost 50 dancers and delivers over 100 annual shows, including full-length and mixed ballets. The Pacific Northwest Ballet has toured across Europe, Hong Kong, Taiwan, Canada, Australia, and the U.S.

The Pacific Northwest Ballet School was established in 1974. Today, it's located next to the Pacific Northwest Ballet at McCaw Hall. It holds a summer course in July annually and is recognized for being one of the strongest courses in the country. The company is renowned for performing the Maurice Sendak *Nutcracker* from 1983 to 2014. Additionally, it was turned into a feature film. They were selected to perform in multiple important festivals for the ballet industry in 2006. Today, you can select one of their amazing productions to attend for a fantastic night or afternoon out.

Best Time to Visit: The Pacific Northwest Ballet is open Monday through Friday from 10:00 a.m. to 6:00 p.m.

Pass/Permit/Fees: Tickets for the Pacific Northwest Ballet start at $30 per person.

Physical Address:
Pacific Northwest Ballet
301 Mercer Street
Seattle, WA 98109

GPS Coordinates: 47.62452° N, 122.35146° W

Did You Know? The Pacific Northwest Ballet performs at McCaw Hall at the Seattle Center, which is the same location used by the Seattle Opera.

Seattle Whale Watching Tours

Seattle Whale Watching Tours are an excellent way to spend a few hours out on the water. You'll learn some interesting facts about the type of whale you're looking for, conservation efforts, and how to safely observe marine animals.

In March and April, you can view the migration of the gray whale to Alaska. These whales can reach up to 50 feet and live up to 70 years. During these two months, they take a detour from their journey to rest and fuel up in the Salish Sea. From May to October, the objective changes to observing orca and humpback whales. You'll spend half a day on a journey to view these magnificent creatures. The trip will last three to five hours depending on where the captain takes the boat.

Best Time to Visit: The Seattle Gray Whale Watching Tour is available on weekends in March and April from 11 a.m. to 2 p.m. The half-day Seattle Whale Watching Tour is available from 10:30 a.m. to 3:30 p.m. daily during the period of May 12 through September 10. From September 15 to October 8, it is only available from Friday through Sunday.

Pass/Permit/Fees: The ticket prices for the Seattle Gray Whale Watching Tour start at $80. The Seattle Whale Watching Tour starts at $109.

Physical Address:
Clipper Vacations
2701 Alaskan Way, Pier 69
Seattle, WA 98121

GPS Coordinates: 48.69458° N, 122.15899° W

Did You Know? You may see both mammal-eating and salmon-eating orca whales on your trip. However, if the captain or guides notice a salmon-eating orca, the boat will be directed away according to regulations. As of January 2021, only 71 of these whales were left in existence.

Seattle Free Walking Tours

Seattle Free Walking Tours offers several options for getting out and about on foot in the city. The best part is that most of the tours they offer are free, as their name indicates. They have a few specialty tours that cost money, but the rest are on a donate-as-you-will policy. The Seattle 101 tour is an excellent choice for those who are in the city for the first time. This two-hour trek that will show you excellent sights, including architecture, things to do, and historical points of interest. The Market Experience will take you through Pike Place Market.

While you can explore the city independently, why not let a guide take you through and point out everything you'd likely miss without help? There's also a paid version of the Market Experience in which you can sample the delectable foods at favorite local restaurants in Pike Place Market. Another premium paid tour is the Old Seattle Cemetery Tour where you can see many famous landmarks, including the Bruce Lee and Brandon Lee graves and the Denny Family Monument.

Best Time to Visit: Seattle Free Walking Tours operates Friday through Monday from 9:00 a.m. to 3:00 p.m.

Pass/Permit/Fees: Seattle Free Walking Tours have free admission. The Insider's Market Experience costs $49.99 per person, and the Old Cemetery Tour costs $20 per person.

Physical Address:
Seattle Free Walking Tours
2001 Western Avenue (Totem Poles)
Seattle, WA 98121

GPS Coordinates: 47.60801° N, 122.33942° W

Did You Know? Seattle Free Walking Tours is the only company of its kind in Seattle.

The Center for Wooden Boats

The Center for Wooden Boats is focused on maintaining and cataloging the region's historical boating record. The museum was founded in the 1970s by Dick Wagner. Since then, it has expanded into three locations. There are more than 170 vessels in the collection at the Center for Wooden Boats. Most of them are sailboats and rowboats, and the collection is divided into several sections.

A livery fleet includes rowboats, daysailers, and pedal boats. The Blanchard Junior Knockabout, a 20-footer, is the primary vessel of the rental fleet at the Center for Wooden Boats. The Blanchard Boat Company located on Lake Union designed and constructed these boats. The museum has eight of these vessels, which are used specifically for teaching and rental purposes. You'll find a hands-on learning experience when you visit the museum. They allow visitors to take part in boat restorations to learn the processes. In addition, you can learn how to build a boat or take part in woodworking classes.

Best Time to Visit: The Center for Wooden Boats is open Wednesday through Sunday from 10:00 a.m. to 6:00 p.m.

Pass/Permit/Fees: Kayaks and canoes can be rented for $35 per hour, rowboats for $40 per hour, small sailboats for $50 per hour, and large sailboats for $100 per hour. Admission to The Center for Wooden Boats facility is free.

Physical Address:
The Center for Wooden Boats
1010 Valley Street
Seattle, WA 98109

GPS Coordinates: 47.62675° N, 122.33652° W

Did You Know? The Center for Wooden Boats includes a living exhibit of boats in the water. These include boats they have refurbished and now include in their fleet.

Hot Tub Boats

In 2011, the founder and creator of Hot Tub Boats developed the idea for the model. He was on his houseboat freezing, wishing he had a hot tub for its warmth but knowing he could never have one installed on his boat. He started brainstorming about how to create a boat with a hot tub built in. He reached out to some friends, and they quickly worked together to get the prototype developed. Once they realized it would work, the rest was history.

Today, you can rent a boat with a hot tub installed in it and enjoy LED lights, temperature controls, and Bluetooth speakers. With the temperature controls, you can cool things down in the summer and keep it warm and toasty in the winter, making this a year-round option for something fun to do in Seattle. An easy-to-use control stick on each boat allows you to drive it where you want to go. You can navigate Lake Union, viewing sights like Gasworks Park and the skyline. The hot tub boats are rated as safe for up to six passengers by the U.S. Coast Guard. Once you return to shore, Hot Tub Boats has hot showers with all the self-care necessities ready for you.

Best Time to Visit: Hot Tub Boats is open every day from 8 a.m. to 11 p.m., rain or shine.

Pass/Permit/Fees: Rentals at Hot Tub Boats are $400 for 2 hours. They require a $150 deposit that will be charged to your card when you are within 7 days of your rental date.

Physical Address:
Hot Tub Boats
2520 Westlake Avenue North
Seattle, WA 98109

GPS Coordinates: 47.64314° N, 122.34313° W

Did You Know? A completely filled hot tub boat holds 2,500 pounds of water. Because of the hot tub's central positioning, the heavy weight of the water does not affect the balance or stability of the boat.

Moss Bay

If you're looking for access to the water, Moss Bay can get you out on Lake Union. With rentals for paddleboards and kayaks, you can explore the lake and see the sights while enjoying the lovely weather. They don't offer reservations, so you'll need to be prompt if the weather is exceptionally nice because they may have a waitlist to get equipment.

Moss Bay also offers tours for both adults and children. Children will receive a brief lesson and then be guided around the lake for an hour and a half. Adults will have a two-hour tour.

Best Time to Visit: Moss Bay is open from April through October. Hours vary by season, but opening and closing times are usually around 10:00 a.m. and 6:00 p.m., respectively. Moss Bay stays open the longest in the summer when it closes at 8:00 p.m.

Pass/Permit/Fees: Paddleboard rentals are $24 per hour. Single kayak rentals are $24 per hour, and double kayak rentals are $32 per hour. Children's kayak tours are $35, and adults kayak tours are $75.

Physical Address:
Moss Bay
1001 Fairview Avenue North, #1900
Seattle, WA 98109

GPS Coordinates: 47.62946° N, 122.33182° W

Did You Know? The waterways have a seven-knot speed limit, so anything you rent from Moss Bay will be safe and comfortable to head out on the water.

Proper Planning

With this guide, you are well on your way to properly planning a marvelous adventure. When you plan your travels, you should become familiar with the area, save any maps to your phone for access without internet, and bring plenty of water—especially during the summer months. Depending on which adventure you choose, you will also want to bring snacks or even a lunch. For younger children, you should do your research and find destinations that best suit your family's needs. You should also plan when and where to get gas, local lodgings, and food. We've done our best to group these destinations based on nearby towns and cities to help make planning easier.

Dangerous Wildlife

There are several dangerous animals and insects you may encounter while hiking. With a good dose of caution and awareness, you can explore safely. Here are steps you can take to keep yourself and your loved ones safe from dangerous flora and fauna while exploring:

- Keep to the established trails.
- Do not look under rocks, leaves, or sticks.
- Keep hands and feet out of small crawl spaces, bushes, covered areas, or crevices.
- Wear long sleeves and pants to keep arms and legs protected.
- Keep your distance should you encounter any dangerous wildlife or plants.

Limited Cell Service

Do not rely on cell service for navigation or emergencies. Always have a map with you and let someone know where you are and how long you intend to be gone, just in case.

First Aid Information

Always travel with a first aid kit in case of emergencies.

Here are items you should be certain to include in your primary first aid kit:

- Nitrile gloves
- Blister care products
- Band-Aids in multiple sizes and waterproof type
- Ace wrap and athletic tape
- Alcohol wipes and antibiotic ointment
- Irrigation syringe
- Tweezers, nail clippers, trauma shears, safety pins
- Small zip-lock bags containing contaminated trash

It is recommended to also keep a secondary first aid kit, especially when hiking, for more serious injuries or medical emergencies. Items in this should include:

- Blood clotting sponges
- Sterile gauze pads
- Trauma pads
- Second-skin/burn treatment
- Triangular bandages/sling
- Butterfly strips
- Tincture of benzoin
- Medications (ibuprofen, acetaminophen, antihistamine, aspirin, etc.)
- Thermometer

- CPR mask
- Wilderness medicine handbook
- Antivenin

There is much more to explore, but this is a great start.

For information on all national parks, visit https://www.nps.gov/index.htm .

This site will give you information on up-to-date entrance fees and how to purchase a park pass for unlimited access to national and state parks. This site will also introduce you to all of the trails at each park.

Always check before you travel to destinations to make sure there are no closures. Attractions may change their hours or temporarily shut down for various reasons. Check the websites for the most up-to-date information.

Made in the USA
Las Vegas, NV
13 January 2024